Health & Safety Curriculum

Primary

by
Max W. Fischer

Published by Instructional Fair
an imprint of
Frank Schaffer Publications®

Instructional Fair

Author: Max W. Fischer
Editors: Elizabeth Flikkema, Lisa Hancock
Cover Artist: Darcy Myers

Frank Schaffer Publications®

Instructional Fair is an imprint of Frank Schaffer Publications.

Send all inquiries to:
Frank Schaffer Publications
8720 Orion Place
Columbus, Ohio 43240

Health & Safety Curriculum—primary

ISBN: 1-56822-289-0

7 8 9 10 11 12 PAT 11 10 09

Table of Contents

Introduction

Health is *the subject* that will accompany every student each and every day, in and out of school. Very likely, it will be the most vital component of their lives.

The better we educate young students about health and the lifestyles and habits that lead to good health, the more they will realize its benefits in adulthood. *Health and Safety Curriculum* is designed to promote stimulating lessons for primary students. Using simulations, problem-solving vignettes, motivating demonstrations, and creative review activities, *Health and Safety Curriculum* offers numerous avenues of learning for students. Its twenty-seven lessons engage students with such diverse topics as nutrition, home safety, substance abuse, and more.

This book attempts to stimulate student interest in a subject area that is often overlooked due to a lack of innovative materials and lesson plans. *Health and Safety Curriculum* is dedicated to the belief that the lessons with the greatest influence on health are those that are internalized through a proactive hands-on approach.

Controlling Stress

Objective

Students will identify at least two ways they can help reduce harmful stress in their lives.

Background

Adrenaline is the hormone produced during moments of extreme stimulation. It provides the body with greater strength or energy. Riding a roller coaster, playing a baseball game or being asked to spell a word in front of the class are typical examples of when our body has a temporary increase in energy requirements.

However, under certain conditions, this helpful internal energy release may become chronic. Divorce, a move to another town, or an inability to organize one's schoolwork may lead to the harmful consequences of stress as outlined in the latter part of step #1 in the *Procedure* section. It is at these times of high anxiety that students need the coping skills of opening up to parents and friends, as well as the physical skills of exercise, sufficient sleep, and proper nutrition in warding off the negative effects of stress.

Materials

- copies of the reading selection and worksheets, "Wired Willy"

Preparation

- Make copies of the reading selection and worksheet for each student.

Procedure

1. Ask students if they have ever been in a running race. Ask them to recall the excitement before the race began. Conclude this introduction by asking if the student(s) would enjoy running a race that lasted every hour they were awake. It can be harmful to the entire body if excitement is ongoing in a person's life. Some stress may be helpful, such as the excitement one would feel just before a race.

Entertain a discussion on stress with the class employing your health text or teacher-led questions. Suggested questions may include, **"What is stress?"** (a feeling of tension or strain on your mind and/or body) **"Have you ever felt stress?"** (Answers will vary.) **"How can stress affect your body?"** (The heart may beat faster; the palms of the hand may get sweaty, breathing may quicken to gain more oxygen for the body; and stored sugar may be released to allow for more energy.)

"Can stress be helpful?" (Yes.) **"How?"** (It can help one do his/her best when he/she feels occasional pressure, such as competing in a ballgame or race or doing well on a test. It can give one an energy lift.)

"How can stress be harmful?" (Stress can be harmful when events occur in one's life that cause prolonged tension or worry. This may lead to restlessness, a lack of sleep, nervousness, headaches, the heart working faster, and an inability of the body to fight off disease. Over a long period of time, it could damage the heart.)

"How can one control stress?" (talking and sharing feelings with your parents and friends, getting enough exercise and rest, eating a balanced diet)

For more information, see *Background*.

2. Have the students read the story and answer the subsequent questions on the "Wired Willy" worksheet. This may be done individually, in small groups, or with the entire class.

Answers to Worksheet:

1. at the start of the game
2. when he blamed himself for the loss
3. not sharing his feelings of guilt with his parents or friends
4. assignments weren't completed; he appeared tired during class
5. probably not; answers will vary
6. talking with his parents helped Willy understand the problem
7. talking with parents and friends about important issues in your life; getting enough sleep and exercise; eating a balanced diet

Wired Willy

Read the story and answer the questions that follow.

Willy felt like he had butterflies in his stomach as the basketball game was about to begin. He wanted to do his best against this champion team. When the game started, Willy forgot all about being anxious and played very well. He led his team in scoring in this Midget League championship game.

With one second left in the game, Willy was fouled while shooting the ball. His team was behind by two points. With two free throws, Willy had a chance to tie the game. Willy made his first shot but missed the second. Willy's team lost by one point. Willy felt horrible. He believed that he was responsible for the loss.

Not wanting to talk to anyone after the game, Willy hurried home. He went to his room and refused to talk to his parents about the game. In his distress, he even forgot about his school project that was due the next day. All he thought about was missing the last shot. His stomach hurt and he had a difficult time getting to sleep that night.

The next day, Willy ignored his friends who wanted to talk about the game. He yawned frequently and almost fell asleep in class. Because his project wasn't completed, his teacher wasn't pleased. In fact, for several days, Willy had a hard time getting any of his schoolwork done and he seemed very tired.

Willy's parents encouraged him to talk about what was bothering him. Willy finally shared how he thought he had lost the game for his team. His parents helped him realize that without Willy's strong effort, his team would not have been so close to winning in the first place. They also reminded him that the reason for playing was not just winning. Someone had to lose. Willy slept much better that night when he realized he had done his best, and that was all anyone could do.

Wired Willy (Cont.)

IF8499 Health & Safety

1. When did Willy feel helpful stress in this story? _____

_____

2. What caused Willy to start feeling harmful stress? _____

_____

3. What created more harmful stress for Willy? _____

_____

4. How did Willy's schoolwork suffer because of increased stress? _____

_____

5. Do you think Willy was pleasant to be around during this time? Explain.

_____

_____

6. What finally helped Willy successfully deal with his stress? _____

_____

7. Name three ways that you can help control harmful stress. _____

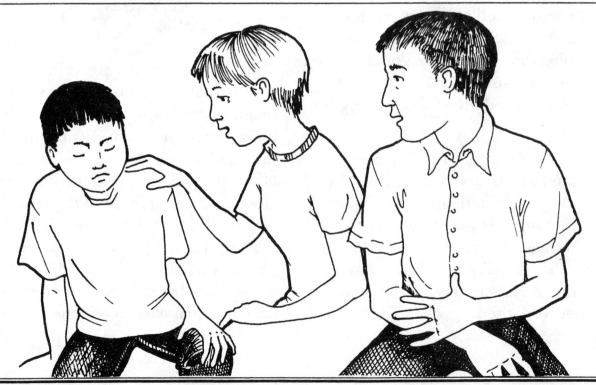

Self-Image

Objective

Students will improve their self-image by discovering and promoting their special interests or skills.

Background

Self-image is a major determining factor in how successful a person is. A person who believes in him/herself, can achieve more than one who doesn't. It is not a lesson that can be easily taught or learned in one sitting. Neither is it something you learn from a book. Self-image is the cumulative product of one's life experiences and attitudes.

The poster activity, "A Star Is Born," is an opportunity for students to inventory those things at which they excel or take pleasure in.

Materials

- one sheet of 12" x 18" white or colored construction paper for each student
- rulers
- assorted crayons and markers
- magazines for cutting out pictures (optional)
- safety scissors (optional)
- student-supplied photographs (optional)
- a movie poster (optional)

Preparation

Obtain the various materials. (You might try the local cinema in obtaining a movie poster of a past film.)

In advance, invite students to bring in photos of themselves.

Procedure

1. If you have a movie poster, share it with the class. Be sure to note how the poster tries to grab your attention (bold lettering, bright colors, etc.), and how it promotes the actors by illustrating an exciting scene.

2. Explain to the class that they will be creating movie posters. The movie they will be advertising will be about themselves. Provide instruction on using a ruler to make neat lettering on a poster.

3. In a large or small group, generate ideas to get students thinking about what they like to do. They should include some of their interests or skills: playing ball, collecting baseball cards, ballet, music, roller skating, etc., in the poster. Students can add a title using their own name or one that tells about something they are accomplished at doing. They can use photos of themselves, pictures from magazines, as well as their own art work. The poster should grab people's attention by advertising the students as stars.

4. Pass out the paper and rulers.

Curriculum Integration

Students may be interested in reading about successful individuals who believed in themselves. There are many examples of people who have overcome apparently insurmountable physical limitations and/or social obstacles. The following is a partial list for review:

Ludwig von Beethoven

Wilma Rudolph

Glenn Cunningham

Mel Tillis

Thomas Edison

Stevie Wonder

Helen Keller

Ronnie Milsap

Jackie Robinson

Teacher Notes

_____

_____

_____

_____

_____

_____

_____

_____

_____

_____

Food Pyramid

Objective

Students will become familiar with the food pyramid. They will identify those food groups from which they need to obtain the majority of their daily nutritional needs. They will identify the food group from which they need the least amount of daily servings.

Background

Primary-age students need "hands-on" experiences to construct their knowledge. They develop concepts best when provided with concrete learning opportunities.

This lesson uses manipulatives to serve as the concrete basis for the students' comprehension of the need for a balanced diet.

Materials

- a set of from 300 to 500 multi-colored, plastic, interlocking, cubic centimeter cubes (often part of math manipulative kits)
- an overhead transparency of the accompanying USDA food pyramid
- an overhead transparency of a recent school menu
- pictures of various foods (representing all the food groups in the pyramid)
- four different colors of markers
- an overhead projector
- copies of the student worksheet

Preparation

- Obtain the plastic cubes, food pictures, markers, overhead projector, and a recent school menu.
- Make copies of the school menu and accompanying food pyramid and worksheet for each student. Make transparencies of the food pyramid and school menu at this time.
- Get the help of students to sort the cubes into the cups. Give each pair of students 25 plastic interlocking cubes—12 of one color, 8 of a second color, 4 of a third, and 1 of a fourth color. (These colors should correspond to the four colors of markers you have chosen.)

Procedure

1. With students working in pairs, distribute the sets of interlocking cubes and instruct them to use the cubes to build a structure following these guidelines: The color grouping of twelve should be snapped together to form a flat, bottom layer. The color grouping of eight should be added on as a second layer. The color grouping of four should be the third layer, while the single-colored cube should be placed at the very top.

2. After their structures are completed, ask students if they recognize the basic structure. (Pyramid) Have them lay the pyramid on different sides on their desktops. **"Which arrangement of the pyramid gives it the best chance of not falling over?"** (the twelve color cube side on the desktop) **"Is there a greater chance of it tipping over if the single cube is on the bottom or top?"** (bottom) **"Why?"** (It has only one block to rest on.)

3. Show the food pyramid transparency on the overhead. Explain to the class that our food needs are similar to a pyramid. On a daily basis, we need more of certain types of foods than of others. In fact, with some food types we need very little. If you relied too much on the foods with small sections in the pyramid, your health would have a good chance of letting you down just as the pyramid falls down if stood on its top. With the transparency, explain the food groups, give examples and the approximate number of daily servings required. (Note that the number of servings may vary depending on individual requirements of age, size and amount of activity.) Outline each level of the pyramid with the colored marker that corresponds to the color of the plastic cubes the students used in making their pyramids. This is vital in helping younger students make a transference from a concrete idea (the pyramid they built) to the abstract food pyramid. Have students outline their pyramids in the same colors.

4. Display the food pictures one at a time to the class. Ask students where on the pyramid each

would fit. Some may fit in two categories.

5. Distribute the school menus. Have student pairs look at a three-day section of that menu. Make sure the same three days are being used by the entire class. Have each student write the names of each food listed on the menu of those days in the appropriate food group box on their worksheet.

Allow students to check their own work as the teacher leads a discussion reviewing each menu item. A balanced diet will have foods written in all the boxes, with progressively more listed as you move down the pyramid. Discuss whether the school provides a balanced menu. Where is it lacking?

As a final review, have each student complete the worksheet, "Pyramid Power."

For an extension, have students study the "Taste/Smell Diagram" on page 14. Have students draw their own diagram surrounded by favorite food pyramid foods. Students may also write the food pyramid group to which each food belongs.

Answers to Worksheet:

1. grains—4 to 6 ounces; meat and beans—3 to 5 ounces; milk and milk equivalents—2 to 3 cups; fruits—1 to 1 ½ cups; vegetables– 1 ½ to 2 ½ cups; oils—use sparingly (4 to 5 teaspoons)

2. Answers will vary.

3. breads and cereals

4. oils—Oils may cause excess weight gain. Foods from this group do not provide any nutrients.

Curriculum Integration

Have students work in teams to draw a large pyramid on butcher paper to represent the USDA's food pyramid. Students could draw and paint or use pictures of appropriate foods in each food group's box.

Teacher Notes

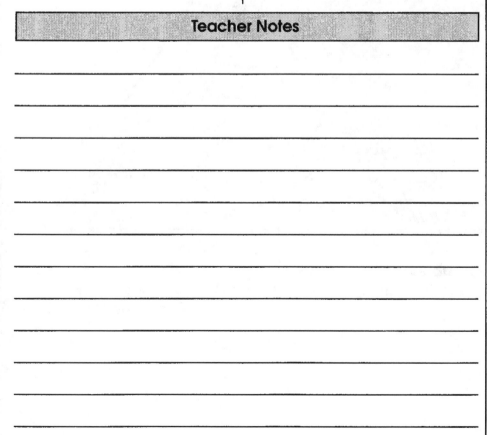

Name _____

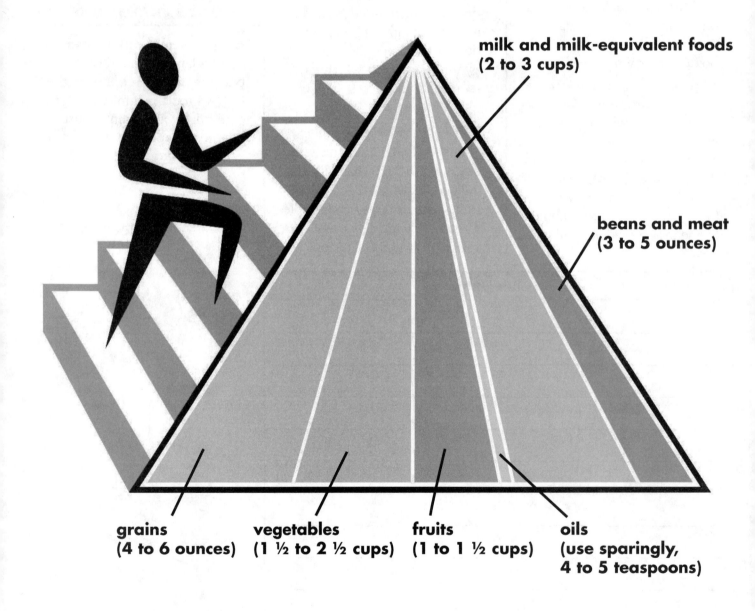

milk and milk-equivalent foods
(2 to 3 cups)

beans and meat
(3 to 5 ounces)

grains
(4 to 6 ounces)

vegetables
(1 ½ to 2 ½ cups)

fruits
(1 to 1 ½ cups)

oils
(use sparingly,
4 to 5 teaspoons)

Pyramid Power

Use your knowledge of the different food groups to answer the following questions.

1. Name all the food groups listed on the food pyramid and give the suggested number of daily servings.

   _____   _____

   _____   _____

   _____   _____

2. Name your favorite food from each of the food groups listed above.

   _____   _____

   _____   _____

   _____

3. From which food group should you regularly eat the most foods?

   _____

4. From which food group should you eat the least food? Why? _____

   _____

   _____

Taste/Smell Diagram

Taste combines with smell to help give many foods their flavor. Taste and smell are relayed to the brain by nerves from sensory cells located in the tongue and nose.

Temperature also affects a food's taste; the taste receptors are more sensitive to food temperatures of 85°–105°F.

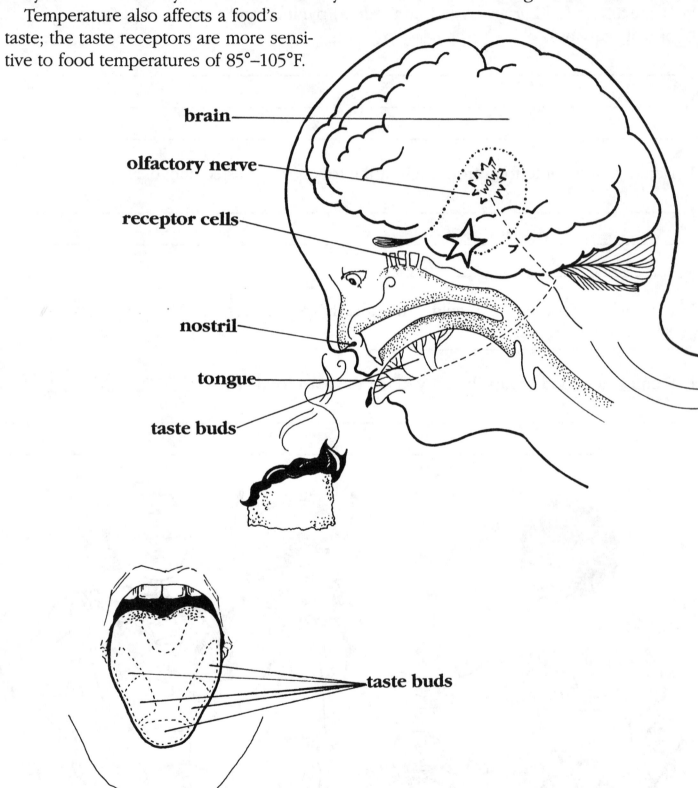

brain

olfactory nerve

receptor cells

nostril

tongue

taste buds

taste buds

Food Groups

Objective

Students will identify and match foods from the same food groups.

Background

"Food Dominoes" is designed for young students to get acquainted with the basic food groups. The teacher could explain the game by making some sample plays on the overhead. The object is for students to match foods from the same food groups using the food pyramid for reference. Groups of students could then play as a class activity, or individual groups could play when other work has been completed.

Materials

- the accompanying "Food Dominoes" sheets
- overhead transparencies of the dominoes for demonstration (optional)
- an overhead projector (optional)

Preparartion

- Copy a set of "Food Dominoes" for each group of four students.
- Make an overhead transparency of one set. (optional)
- Cut out the dominoes. Older students may be able to do this on their own.
- Laminate for greater durability.

Procedure

1. Each domino has two parts, each part representing a separate food group. Five dominoes are doubles in which foods of the same food group appear on both sides. The double *multi-food* domino is always put aside as the starter for the game. The remaining dominoes are shuffled or mixed and turned facedown. Each player picks out five and turns them faceup in front of him/her.

2. After the double *multi-food* domino has been placed in the center of the playing area, the first player may place one of his/her dominoes to one end of the double domino if the picture matches. The second player may try to match the double domino or the food end on the other end of the second domino played. The play continues with the third and fourth players. Only one domino may be played at each turn. Dominoes are played lengthwise instead of at right angles. The only exception to this rule is in the case of doubles (both ends represent the same food group), where right angles are permitted.

3. A double is always played crosswise to the end it matches. This creates two new directions in which the dominoes may be played.

4. If a player cannot make a match, he/she must draw from the remaining, facedown dominoes until he/she is able to play. If he/she draws the last remaining domino and is still unable to play, he/she must "pass" and try again on his/her next turn.

5. The first player to use all of his/her dominoes wins. Or, if no further plays can be made, the player with the least number of dominoes left wins the game.

Teacher Notes

_____

_____

_____

_____

_____

_____

_____

_____

_____

_____

_____

_____

_____

_____

_____

_____

_____

Food Dominoes

Name _____

 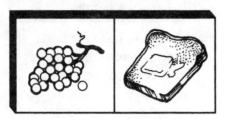 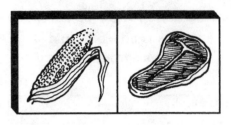

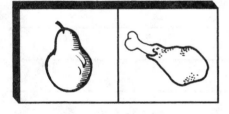  

 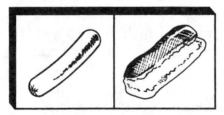 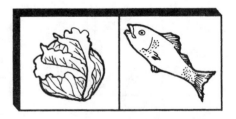

Balanced Diet

Objective

Students will become aware that overindulgence of non-nutritious foods may have a negative effect upon their health and appearance.

Background

Diets loaded with excess fat and sugar can be harmful in several ways. Making poor judgments about these types of foods can lead to excessive weight gain and, in the case of sugar, poor dental health. Sugars combine with bacteria to create acids that attack tooth enamel and introduce cavities.

Primary grade students are already well on their way to forming habits that will carry them through adolescence and into adulthood. The use of hyperbole in the "Self Portrait" worksheet is designed to help students realize the effects too much fat and sugar can have on their health.

Materials

- drawing paper
- crayons or colored pencils
- copies of the worksheet

Preparation

- Make one copy of the worksheet for each student.
- Obtain the other materials.

Procedure

1. The activity should accompany a lesson which stresses the reasons to eat limited amounts of fatty or sugary foods. (See *Background*.)

2. Have the students divide their drawing paper in half. On one half, have them draw a self-portrait of how they think they look at the present time. Have them title this drawing "As I Am Today."

3. Pass out the worksheet and instruct the students to read each of the selections. (The teacher may read aloud as the students follow along silently.) Discuss with the class the unusual nature of each diet. Refer to the food pyramid in the class discussion.

4. After reading all the selections, have each student choose one and imagine that their diet for the next year would be similar to that described. Even though the story described just one meal, explain to the students that the foods mentioned would be the only kinds of food they would eat each and every day for a year. Every breakfast, lunch, and dinner would consist of only these types of foods. Ask students what they think a person would look like after a year of eating this way.

5. On the other half of their drawing sheet, students will now draw what they think they would probably look like after a year's worth of eating an improper diet (according to the story they've chosen).

6. After students have finished their "before" and "after" drawings, allow them a forum in which to share their portraits. They could share in small groups, as a whole class, or one-on-one with the teacher. The teacher could use the drawings to evaluate whether or not students had acquired knowledge of the cause/effect relationship between types of foods and physical condition.

Answers to Worksheet:

1. fatty and/or sugary foods
2. fruits, vegetables, whole grains
3. No, this is not a balanced diet. Several of the food groups are missing.

Curriculum Integration

Have students use their math skills to total the quantity of the sugary and fatty foods each of these story characters would eat in a week (if the story represents one of three "normal" daily meals).

Older students may include liquid measure when dealing with cans of soda or cups of maple-flavored syrup. Cups may be compared to the liquid volume of cans. (One cup = 8 ounces; most soda cans hold 12 ounces of beverage.)

Self-Portrait

Ricky Fingerlicker was enjoying his breakfast. He had a piece of white toast spread with butter and covered with a cup of maple-flavored syrup. On the side, he had a bowl of "Sweet Treats" cold cereal. He had added three heaping spoonfuls of sugar because it wasn't sweet enough. He stuffed himself further with six chocolate-covered doughnuts, and washed everything down with two glasses of sweetened Kool Aid.

Adam Greasespot couldn't wait for supper. After all, he hadn't eaten in two hours. The menu included sausage and pepperoni pizza, with extra cheese, resting in a pool of grease. Adam knew he could eat seven dripping pieces by himself and still have room for dessert—"Triple Treat"—peanut butter-marshmallow-chocolate ice cream covered with hot fudge sauce and whipped cream.

Lisa Lipsmacker sat down to her typical homemade lunch. First, she had a butter sandwich—five thick pats of butter between two thin pieces of white bread. Her second sandwich was her favorite, peanut butter and fried bologna. On the side, she had a picnic-size bag of potato chips with French onion dip and two cans of cola.

Choose one of the stories and answer the following questions.

1. What kinds of food is this person eating a lot of? _____

_____

2. What important types of foods are missing from his/her diet? _____

_____

3. Is this a good, balanced diet? Why or why not? _____

_____

Awareness of Fat

Objective

Students will identify foods with excessive amounts of fat.

Background

With recent studies indicating that a large portion of Americans are obese (defined as being over twenty percent beyond their recommended body weight for their height and sex), it becomes imperative to warn primary students of the potential dangers of too much fat in their diets. "Grease Detective" is intended to help students take the first step in combating obesity and its associated ills by recognizing the common foods that contribute to obesity.

Materials

- a pat of butter
- a roll of waxed paper
- copies of the food collage worksheet
- an assortment of fatty and non-fatty foods—bologna, hard salami, salad dressing, celery, broccoli, an apple, an orange
- facial tissues

Preparation

- Make one copy of the worksheet for each student.
- Obtain the butter, assorted foods, tissues, and waxed paper.

Procedure

1. Explain to the students that fat is required in our daily diets in very limited amounts. Too much fat can lead to excessive weight gain and, over a prolonged period of time, to a number of diseases due to being overweight—heart disease being one of the most common. Very often we can recognize fatty foods just by their feel and texture. Usually fatty foods will leave clues about what they're made from. Explain to students that these clues can be used to search out fatty foods before we eat too much of them.

2. Display the various food samples so that all students can easily observe them. While holding each food individually, ask the class to raise their hands if they feel the food is considered fatty. Record the survey results on the chalkboard or overhead for later reference.

3. Tear off a sheet of wax paper. Drag one end of the butter across the wax paper. Have the students observe that the butter leaves a greasy trail on the wax paper. You may have one or two students touch the butter trail to verify that fact. (Have students wipe off their greasy fingers with the tissues.) Discuss the point that butter is made up totally of fat. Foods that contain excessive fat will usually leave a greasy trail on wax paper.

4. Have students work as "grease detectives" in teams of two to four. Equip each team with a sheet of waxed paper, tissues, and small portions of assorted food items. Allow the teams to investigate the potential trail of grease for each food, recording their results. When groups have completed their research, compare the results with the initial class survey. You may choose to manage this activity as a demonstration.

5. Distribute the copies of the worksheet and have students mark an *X* on all foods they believe to be fatty. Use the results of this activity and prior knowledge to help make the judgements.

Answers to Worksheet: The following would be considered foods with excessive amounts of fat: salami, doughnut, butter, bologna, salad dressing, mayonnaise, french fries, potato chips, corn chips, and hamburger.

Note: When reviewing the answers, be sure to reassure students that it is all right to eat these foods, but eating them in limited amounts is best for good health.

Grease Detective

Name _____

Place an **X** on any of the pictured foods that contain a large amount of fat.

Fat Comparisons

Objective

Students will compare the amount of fat in certain common foods to the fat content of a stick of butter.

Background

Some nutritionists are using visual representations to help people understand the amount of fat they consume in their diets. Why not present children with this visual means of understanding nutrition? After all, if adults can't relate to the numerical values of fat grams on nutrition labels, do we honestly think children will?

Here are several typical meals compared in fat grams to butter:

A large cheeseburger, medium fries, and chocolate shake from a national fast-food chain—approx. 75 grams of fat or $^7/_8$ stick of butter.

A sandwich with two slices of bologna or salami with a tablespoon of mayonnaise and $1^1/_4$ oz. of corn chips—approx. 41 grams of fat or $^1/_2$ stick of butter.

Two medium slices of sausage/pepperoni pizza—approx. 46 grams of fat or $^1/_2$ stick of butter (this can vary somewhat depending upon toppings and actual size).

Two hot dogs, $1^1/_4$ oz. of potato chips, and a cream-filled snack cake or chocolate candy bar—approx. 60 grams of fat or roughly $^3/_4$ stick of butter.

Teachers may create other common fatty combinations to serve as examples for their students.

One further note for teachers. Again, the goal of this activity is to create an awareness of the pervasiveness of fat in our diets, not to provoke an alarmist point of view. **Limited** amounts of fatty foods are tolerable for most individuals, but students must realize the inherent dangers of **too much** fat.

Materials

- a quarter-pound stick of butter
- a tablespoon measuring device and a clear measuring cup
- white drawing paper
- a quart (or larger) container of water
- foodcoloring
- scissors (optional), yellow crayons or markers, and glue
- magazine pictures of various common fatty foods
- copies of the worksheet

Preparation

- Obtain all the above supplies
- Add red, green, or blue food coloring to the water.
- Make one copy of the worksheet for each student.

Procedure

1. Facing the class, hold the stick of butter as if it were an ice-cream cone. Ask how many students would enjoy unwrapping a stick of butter and eating it as if it were an ice-cream cone. Ask students why they would not really relish that prospect.

2. Explain that since most people wouldn't like the idea of eating plain butter, they may be surprised that they often eat as if they were eating just butter. Butter is all fat. One stick of butter contains 88 grams of fat.

   Many of the foods we may like to eat contain large amounts of fat. For example, "how many of you would like this much ice cream?" (Place colored water into the clear measuring cup to $^5/_8$ cup line.) "How about some whipped cream on top? One tablespoon? or two?" (Add two tablespoons of water to the cup.) "If you ate one cup of one of the creamier brands of ice cream, topped with two tablespoons of whipped cream, the fat content of this treat would equal that of $^6/_8$ of a stick of butter." (approx. 65 grams)

3. Have students cut out one of the Butter-Stick graphs from the worksheet at this point. Explain that in the example just given, the fat content of the ice-cream dessert is about six-eighths of a stick of butter. Have students color six-eighths

Fat Comparisons (Cont.)

of their graph with yellow crayon or marker.

4. On the drawing paper, students should draw the dessert of ice cream topped with whipped cream (or glue in place a cut-out magazine picture of it). Have the students glue the "Butter Stick Graph" next to the drawing.

5. Repeat steps #2, #3, and #4 for several other food selections outlined in the *Background* section.

Curriculum Integration

• This may be an advantageous time to introduce weights and measures to your students. Incorporating a balance and some plastic mass weights (grams for starters), students can physically handle and relate the abstract concept of 88 grams of fat in a stick of butter. You may also want to work with the smaller standard units of weight (ounces), if you have a set of weights available. Students could bring in sample food labels from home, and it could be noted how both metric and standard units of weight are featured on food package labels.

Experimentation may also be initiated with liquid measure.

Furnish 8-ounce plastic or Styrofoam cups along with plastic tablespoons. Have students use water to calculate how many tablespoons of liquid equal 8 ounces (16, because 1 tablespoon = 1/2 fluid ounce). Depending on what liquid measuring devices you have available, further investigation could point out the relationship between cups, pints, quarts, gallons, and so on.

• Make butter out of whipping cream. Shake a small amount in a baby food jar until it separates.

Teacher Notes

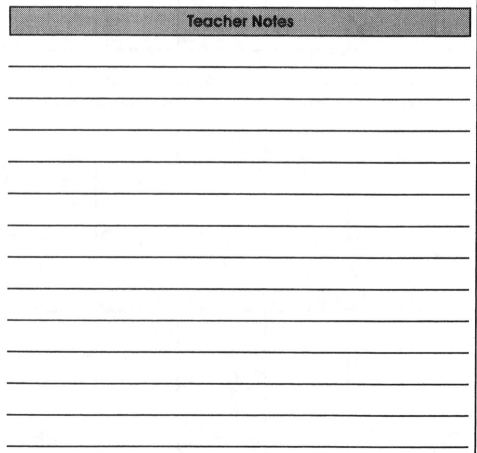

Snackin' on Butter

Butter-Stick Graphs

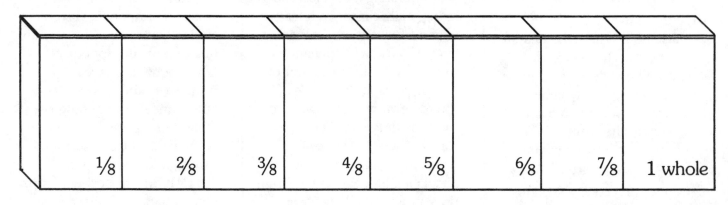

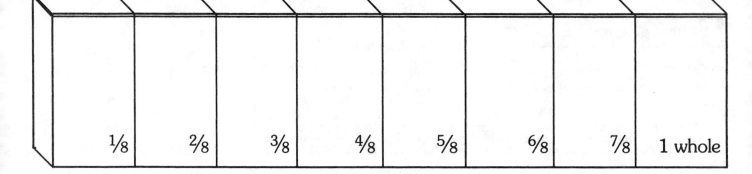

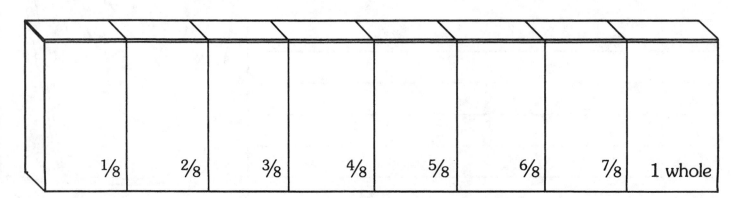

Human Body

Objective

Students will identify the location of the body's major organs.

Background

For young children the actual location of many organs within their bodies is still a mystery. While each may have a general idea of where their stomach lies, they do not comprehend its relative position to the intestines. Likewise, the heart's position to the lungs isn't readily known at this age. "Body Organs" may be used as an anticipatory set to a series of units on body systems. The suggested extension of a full-size display on butcher paper may be completed one organ at a time as different systems are introduced.

Materials

- the accompanying body outline entitled, "Body Organs"
- the accompanying sheet of body organs
- paste, scissors, and crayons
- overhead projector
- "Visible Man (or Woman)" plastic model or overlay chart (optional)
- large sheets of butcher paper (optional)

Preparartion

- Increase the outline of the body by doubling its size, then make copies of the body outline and organ sheets for each student.
- Make transparencies of the body outline and organ sheets.
- Cut out the separate organs from the transparency sheet.

Procedure

1. Divide students into cooperative groups of four. Use a plastic model, chart, or the student's text to discuss the proper location of each organ.

2. Students then cut out and paste each organ in the appropriate location on the body outline. Group members should assist each other in proper placement. The teacher may follow any sequence he/she desires in placing the organs. He/she will use the overhead transparencies to model for students the placement of organs as the lesson progresses.

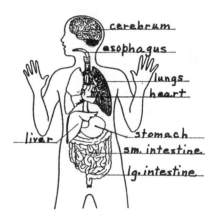

3. Students may color the puzzle for display.

4. A possible extension of this activity would be to have student groups draw full-size body outlines of each other (or of one member of their group) on butcher paper. The group would then draw the various organs where they belong.

Teacher Notes

_____

_____

_____

_____

_____

_____

_____

_____

_____

Body Puzzle

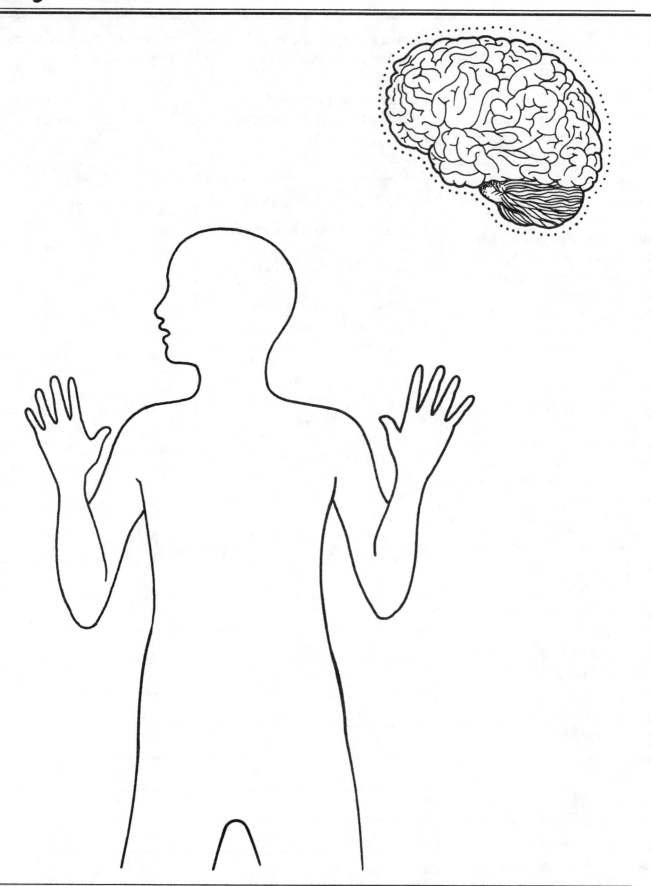

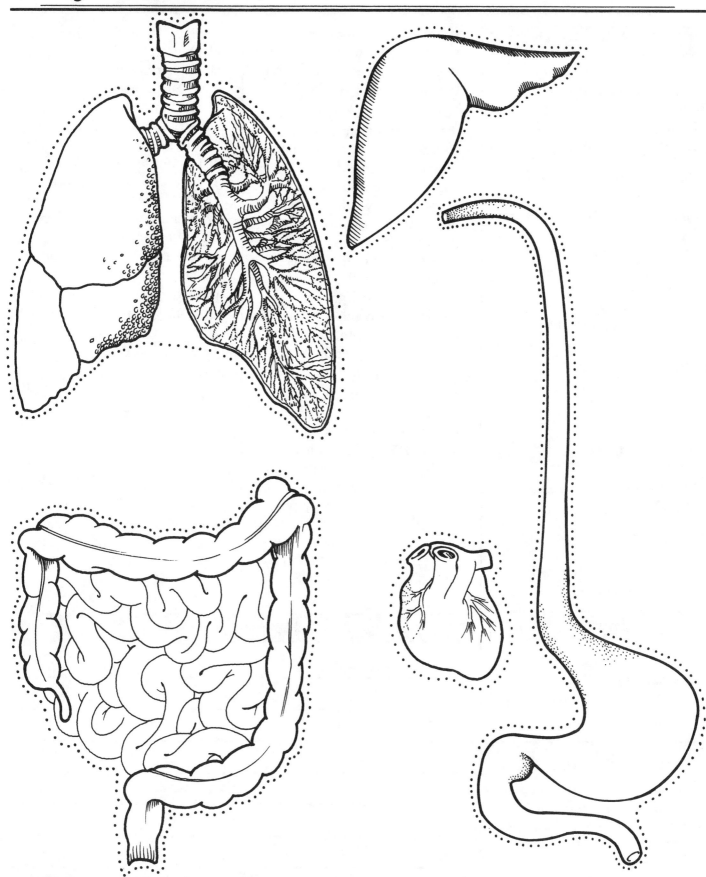

Skeletal System

Objective

Students will identify two ways to build and maintain strong, healthy bones.

Background

The major purpose of this activity is to create awareness and initiate a positive lifetime habit. Osteoporosis, a condition characterized by brittleness and porosity of the bones, affects some people in their later years of life. However, some studies indicate that a life-long regimen of exercise and consumption of calcium will help reduce the possibility of this condition arising.

Materials

- the accompanying worksheet
- a rusty nut and bolt
- a rust-free nut and bolt (perhaps with a drop of lubricating oil on the bolt's threads for even smoother performance)

Preparation

- Make a copy of the worksheet for each student.
- Procure the two different sets of nuts and bolts.

Procedure

Compare a rusty nut and bolt to what might happen to a person's bones when they age. While discussing the skeletal system, use the two sets of nuts and bolts to illustrate the importance of exercise to your bones, especially joints.

1. Have a volunteer try to undo the rusty nut from its bolt. Explain, "This rust has built up over time from little use. The joints between our bones can also become weak from inactivity. A rusty bolt like this will probably break off rather than turn out of the nut as it should. So too, the bones in our body have a greater chance of becoming brittle and breaking without sufficient exercise over the years."

2. Use the clean nut and bolt with a second volunteer. Allow the class to see how easily the nut comes unscrewed. Explain that like this well-oiled nut and bolt assembly, properly maintained bones will serve a body well throughout a lifetime. Ask students to name some different types of exercise that they may do on a regular basis.

3. Explain that another important element in building and maintaining strong, healthy bones is diet. Calcium is an important mineral that our bodies need for proper growth and health. Our bones are made of calcium just as our teeth are. Ask if anyone knows which food group is filled with foods rich in calcium? (dairy) Ask what some of these foods are. (milk, yogurt, cheese, cottage cheese, ice cream)

4. Have students complete the worksheet, "Strong Bones."

5. For an extension, have students do the "Calcium Boosters" worksheet. You may want to supply them with cookbooks and cooking magazines for the activity.

Answers to Worksheet:

1. Answers will vary.

2. milk, cheese, yogurt, cottage cheese, and ice cream

Teacher Notes

_____

_____

_____

_____

_____

_____

Strong Bones

1. List six different activities in which you participated in the last week that could be counted as exercise.

_____   _____

_____   _____

_____   _____

Circle the foods below that will help provide calcium for your growing bones.

Calcium Boosters

Look in cookbooks or magazines for recipes with calcium-rich ingredients. Copy the two that appeal most to you onto the recipe card outlines below. Clip and save for later use.

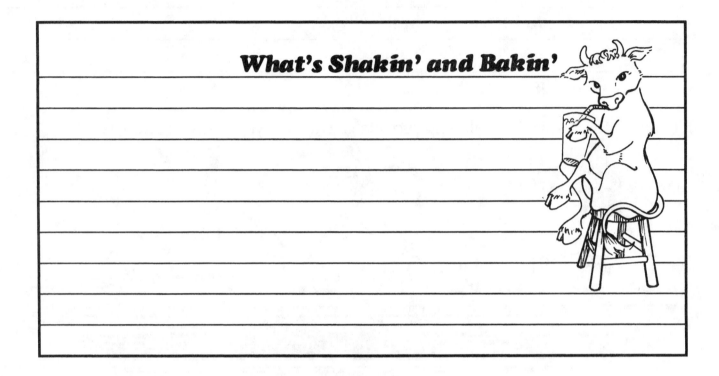

What's Shakin' and Bakin'

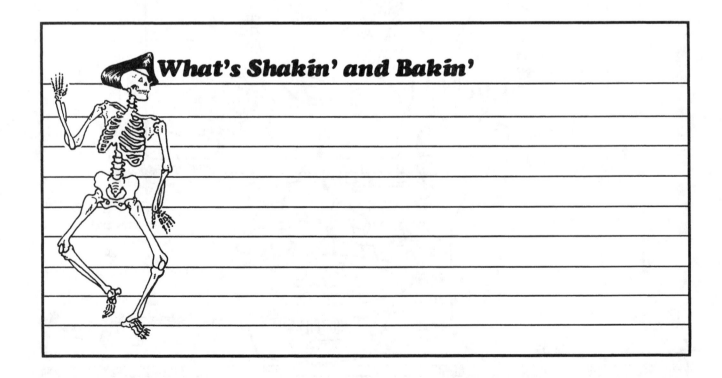

What's Shakin' and Bakin'

Nervous System

Objective

Students will learn how the nervous system operates within the body, how it can be damaged, and three ways of protecting it.

Background

Every time a student hears, sees, tastes, touches, or smells something, his/her nervous system is at work transmitting vital information in a fraction of a second. Connected to the brain stem at the base of the brain, the spinal cord acts as the body's "information super-highway."

Keeping the nervous system healthy should be of paramount importance to anyone, including primary-age students. With the brain located in the head and the spinal cord running down the back from it, the head and neck need constant protection. Properly fitted helmets when bicycling or playing contact football are very important in reducing the risk of head injuries. Avoiding inhaling or ingesting toxic substances, such as household cleaners, glue, illicit drugs and alcohol, or gasoline also protects the nervous system from damage. Students can take measures to protect themselves from head injuries and subsequent damage to the nervous system every time they travel in a car. Buckling seat belts and shoulder harnesses not only saves lives, but it also prevents serious injuries that could possibly paralyze individuals.

Materials

- two (or more) plastic yogurt containers (or wax-coated paper cups)
- about 15 feet of nylon fishing line (enough to stretch across most of the length of the classroom)
- a sewing needle
- several pieces of paper and two pencils
- a large sheet of cardboard, perhaps a flattened large appliance box (optional)
- copies of the worksheet

Preparation

- With the needle, make a small hole in the center of the bottom of each yogurt cup.
- Attach one cup to each end of the fishing line, with cup bottoms facing each other, and make knots to secure the line to each cup.
- Make a copy of the worksheet for each student.

Procedure

1. Select two student volunteers to handle the "telephone" you have made with fishing line and yogurt cups. One person will represent the brain; the other person will represent a specific body part, to begin with, the hand. **Note:** The person in the role of the brain will be the only one actually speaking into one of the cups. Since this could spread germs, choose one student to role-play the brain throughout the activity. The role of the body part is a listening/reacting role which can be easily rotated among several students.

2. Have the two students stand far apart, stretching the "telephone" across the room. They may be seated. The teacher may also place a large cardboard partition somewhere in the middle to block visual contact between the two ends. Explain to the class that the brain is the control center of their entire body. All activity, whether voluntary or involuntary, is initiated here by messages sent through nerves (represented by the fishing line) In this initial activity, the brain is going to tell the hand to write something. Furnish the person in the role of the hand with pencil and paper. The person in the role of the brain will read a message through the telephone for the hand to write. **Note:** The line must be stretched taut in order for the voice vibrations to carry through it. The speaker should not raise his/her voice for this activity to work. Have students note that the hand received the message from the brain.

3. After the successful transmission of the message, have new volunteers replace the "hand,"

Nervous System (Cont.)

taking on the role of the entire body. Write or whisper to the "brain" to send a message for the "body" to raise his/her hand, jump on one leg, or turn around. Make sure that none of these physical commands separates the "telephone" from the listener.

4. After two or three volunteers play the role of the body, send an "obstructed" message. As usual, give the "brain" a written or whispered message to pass on. However, on this occasion, the teacher should position him/herself near the middle of the line and pinch the line together to form a kink. The result of this will be that the transmission is interrupted and the "body" will be unable to receive the brain's message. Explain to the class that when nerves are damaged, messages from the brain may not be able to get through to specific body parts. If the spinal cord, the super-highway of nerves running down the middle of the back from the base of the brain, were damaged, a person could become paralyzed and unable to follow these simple instructions.

5. Discuss ways of protecting your nervous system so that such paralyzing injuries do not occur. Use the *Background* information as a guide for discussion before passing out the worksheet for the students to complete.

Answers to Worksheet:

1. the head/neck
2. wear a properly fitted helmet
3. drugs, alcohol, glue, gasoline, and certain household products
4. wear your seat belt/shoulder harness
5. avoid dangerous stunts especially those that expose your neck to injury

Curriculum Integration

The teacher could set up an interest center on sound, incorporating some basic activities that would give students a better understanding of what sound is, how sound is made, and how to vary it.

- Fill bottles with water to different levels and tap the sides with a variety of objects.
- Watch the vibration of sound in a pan of water.
- Create a straw whistle.
- Make drums and discuss resonance.

Teacher Notes

_____

_____

_____

_____

_____

_____

_____

_____

_____

_____

_____

_____

_____

Message Received

Answer the following questions.

1. What part of your body requires the most protection in order to maintain a healthy nervous system? _____

2. How can you protect your nervous system when you are going bicycle riding?

_____

3. What kinds of substances should you avoid inhaling or eating to keep your nervous system healthy and safe? _____

_____

4. How can you protect your nervous system when you are in your car?

_____

5. In what ways do you think you can protect your nervous system when playing on the playground? _____

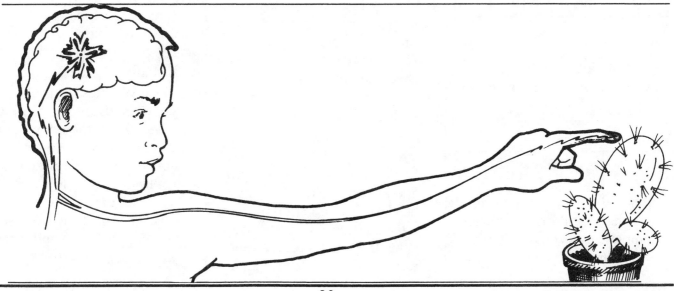

Digestive System

Objective

Students will be able to explain the value of chewing carefully to enhance digestion and derive the greatest benefits from the foods they eat. They will identify the path which most digestion takes from chewing to eliminating.

Background

Digestion begins when saliva in the mouth softens foods while the teeth break them down into suitable sizes for passage through the food tube (esophagus). In the stomach, more digestive juices are added to further break down foods. Nutrients are removed from the food in the small intestine and distributed to the different parts of the body through the blood. The remaining mass of food enters the large intestine where any water is withdrawn and it then prepares to leave the body as waste.

Materials

- two Popsicles
- two rigid plastic straws
- two plastic plates or dishes
- worksheets
- transparency of diagram

Preparation

- Obtain the materials, making sure that one Popsicle remains completely frozen until the activity is presented. The other Popsicle should be allowed to partially thaw before the activity begins. (It should show definite signs of melting—pooling of liquid, the stick becoming loose. It should have the consistency of slush.)
- Make a copy of the worksheets for each student.

Procedure

1. This lesson about digestion of food should begin with discussion about proper eating behaviors. Food should be chewed slowly and swallowed in small amounts (see *Background*). The emphasis of the activity is to imitate the digestive process which takes place in the small intestine.

2. Select two volunteers who will sit at a table. Place a plate with a Popsicle and a straw in front of each student.

3. At a designated signal, have each student try to suction with the straw the liquid from his/her Popsicle.

4. As the activity progresses, it will become obvious that the student cannot drink from the completely frozen Popsicle. Meanwhile, the other student will find the going easier with his/her partially frozen Popsicle.

   Use the overhead and the transparency to explain the parts of the digestive system (page 36). (See *Background*.) Explain to the class that an important part of the digestion of food occurs within the small intestine. The nutrients a food has to offer are siphoned out of liquefied food through finger-like projections within the small intestine. Then the nutrients are carried through the blood to all parts of the body. In the Popsicle demonstration just concluded, the straws represented those projections. The small intestine cannot extract nutrients easily from large chunks of food that have not been properly prepared for digestion. Have a discussion about the importance of chewing food carefully. The partially frozen Popsicle is like food that is easier to digest because it has been broken down and is working its way through the small intestine while providing nutrients for all the body's needs.

5. Use the worksheets, pages 35 and 36, after the discussion and demonstration.

Answers to Worksheet:

a. 1. small intestine 2. mouth 3. esophagus 4. saliva 5. stomach 6. large intestine 7. teeth

b. 1. mouth 2. esophagus 3. small intestine 4. large intestine 5. stomach 6. teeth 7. saliva

Curriculum Integration

The small intestine is about 23 feet (7 meters) long. Since it is coiled within the body cavity, it fits rather nicely. However, students may be amazed to see just how long 23 feet actually is. For an impressive visual, have students take a yardstick or measuring tape and measure off that length in the classroom.

Digestive System

Name _____

_____

Each of the scrambled words makes up a part of your digestive system. Unscramble each word and write it on the blank line.

1. llsma tseninite _____

_____

2. tomuh _____

3. shpoesuga _____

4. lasvai _____

5. hcamots _____

6. ragel enitsetni _____

_____

7. hetet _____

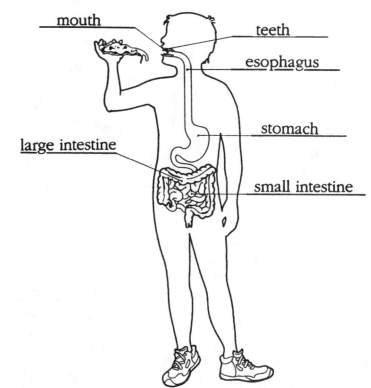

mouth

teeth

esophagus

stomach

large intestine

small intestine

Now match the unscrambled words to their proper descriptions below.

1. This is the part of your body where digestion actually begins. _____

2. This connects your mouth with your stomach. _____

3. Nutrients in food are removed in this part of the digestive system.

_____

4. Water is removed, and waste is stored here. _____

5. Digestive juices are added to food here to help break down food even more.

_____

6. These are used to break food into the right size for swallowing. _____

7. This digestive juice helps begin the digestive process in the mouth. _____

Digestive System

Name _____

Use with page 35.

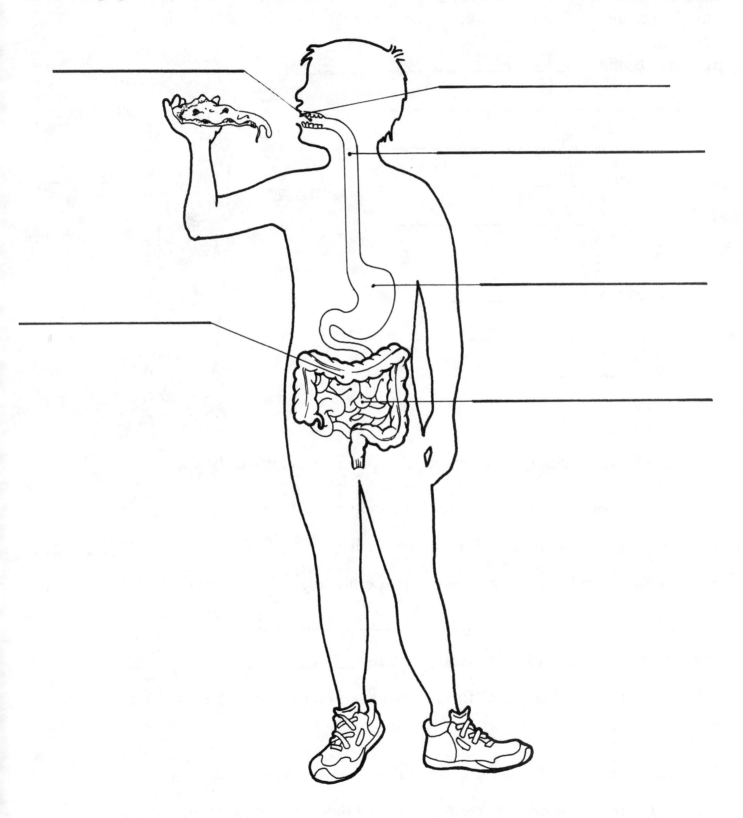

Saying "No!"

Objective

Students will recognize the power in asserting themselves when confronted with possible substance abuse.

Background

This lesson in assertiveness is accompanied by a physical demonstration of how assertiveness strengthens itself with repetition. The worksheet derives its name from an example a wise Native American chief used in describing the Indians' plight against a common enemy. As individual tribes they were relatively powerless. However, as a united body, they would be a more potent force with which to be reckoned. (Discussion of this historic aspect of the activity is optional.) Students are encouraged to develop an arsenal of assertive responses telling why they won't indulge in a harmful substance. The more they practice their response, more powerful their will becomes. Sample responses might include:

My parents won't allow me to do that.

Are you nuts! That's crazy!

No! That is harmful, and I won't become involved with it.

I've seen (heard) what can happen by using that. It's not for me.

No way!

I respect my body too much to

do that to it.

That stuff can kill you! I like living too much.

Assertive behavior includes more than just a set of words. Encourage students to be firm and quick with their rejections of the substance. In fact, the more direct the negative response is to the offer, the faster the situation is dealt with and the easier it becomes for the student to turn his/her back on the solicitation and leave. Help students realize that anyone who would tempt them to harm themselves in such a way is definitely not a friend, no matter how long they may have known them.

Assertiveness should be employed whenever a student believes he/she is being led into a dangerous, unlawful, or unhealthy activity. Teachers should stress that standing up for what is right should not be limited only to situations dealing with substance abuse.

Depending on the age of the students, the teacher may wish to use student volunteers to handle the dowel-breaking demonstration while the teacher supplies the narrative. (Teachers need to wisely judge the appropriateness of having students breaking the dowels. Caution volunteers to hold the dowels away from onlookers.)

Materials

- five 5/16" (or 3/8") wooden dowels, each approx. 18" long

Preparation

- Obtain the dowels, making sure the ends are cut smoothly and that no sharp splinters are present.
- Make a copy of the worksheet for each student.

Procedure

1. Hold one dowel length out in front of you with both hands (thumbs extended toward the middle of the rod).

Explain to the class, that the dowel represents willpower and the ability to say "No!" to using harmful substances such as cigarettes, drugs, or alcohol. (For that matter, it could also represent saying "No!" to overindulgence in any food or drink.)

"If you are tempted by someone to try such a harmful substance for the first time, (slowly and firmly place pressure upon the center of the dowel by pulling the ends in towards you) your will is being tested just as the strength of this dowel is being tested. If one has never said "No!" to this substance before, do you think one's will can

Saying "No!" (Cont.)

withstand the temptation?" (Allow students to offer responses. Their answers may vary.)

2. Continue the even pressure until the dowel breaks in the

middle. **Note:** Be sure to point the dowel away from any individuals before snapping it to prevent any possible splinters from striking someone.

"Because they've never learned to say, 'No!', some people's will will break easily the first time 3. Now take four dowels and stack two on top of the other two. Secure the grouping of dowels at either end with rubber bands.

Hold them out in front of you similar to the way in step #1. "These four dowels represent

someone who has said 'No!' several times before. Do you think it will be easier or harder for their will to be broken this time?" (Allow for student responses.)

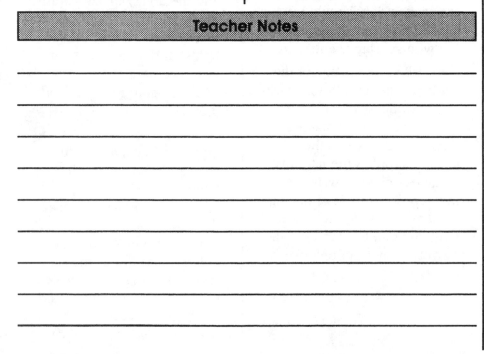

Again, with the thumbs extended toward the middle of the bundle of four dowels, attempt to pull back on the ends (holding the dowels away from students). More than likely, it will be rather difficult to break this remaining bundle.

4. Explain to the class, "By putting these four dowels together it was as if someone had been able to say 'No!' four times to the offer of a dangerous substance. Their will became stronger. That's what happens

each and every time you say 'No!' to a harmful substance such as cigarettes, drugs, or alcohol." (Your will becomes stronger. You become less likely to abuse such a substance. You remain healthier as a result.)

5. Discuss ways to be assertive (see *Background*). Pass out the worksheets. Allow students to work in small groups to write a response to each situation. Team members gain strength from each other as well.

6. Have various groups share their responses with the entire class.

7. Give student groups a situation to role play. Use scenarios such as those on page 39. Have one student tempt, while the others practice firm responses.

Teacher Notes

_____
_____
_____
_____
_____
_____
_____
_____
_____

A Bundle of Arrows

Name _____

Story #1

Charlie was roving the neighborhood with his friends one Saturday morning. On any other Saturday Charlie, Lee, and Tommy would have lots of things to do. However, this particular Saturday the boys weren't quite sure what they were going to do. Tommy gave a sly grin and said, "I've got something that could be very interesting to try." With that, he pulled out a pack of cigarettes along with a book of matches from his coat pocket.

What should Charlie and/or Lee say and do? _____

_____

_____

Story #2

Liz was visiting her new neighbor, Julie, after school one day. They were putting a jigsaw puzzle together in Julie's room. Liz could smell a strong, burning odor. It was like tobacco smoke but not quite the same. She asked if Julie could smell it, too. Julie casually said that it was her older brother smoking marijuana in his bedroom. "It's no big deal," Julie said. " Would you like to smoke some?"

What should Liz say and do? _____

_____

_____

Story #3

Frank and Jerry were walking home from school when they came upon several older boys who were drinking something out of a dark-colored bottle hidden in a paper bag. One of the older boys dared Frank and Jerry to have a drink of beer, "Come on you two, you aren't little babies now are you?"

Jerry looked at Frank and asked, "It couldn't hurt us, could it? Not just a little bit?"

What should Frank do or say in this situation? _____

_____

_____

Smoking

Objective

Students will recognize tar as the sticky, brown, poisonous substance found in cigarettes.

Background

Tar is one of several toxic substances that the federal government has identified in cigarette tobacco. (Others include ammonia, formaldehyde and insecticide.) The tar-stained cotton ball in the following demonstration shows the amount of damage a single cigarette can cause.

Materials

- an empty squeeze bottle (may have contained mustard, ketchup, salad dressing, hair coloring, etc.)
- two cotton balls
- cigarette (filterless, if possible)
- book of matches
- a lid from a jar

Preparation

- Cut the opening in the nozzle of the squeeze bottle large enough to snugly insert the end of a cigarette.

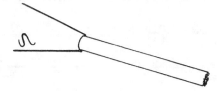

- Unscrew the top and stretch the cotton ball across the top and around the threads like a filter. Secure the cotton ball

by screwing the cap back on the bottle.

- Insert the (filter) end of the cigarette into the opening of the bottle's nozzle.

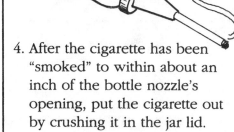

1. After having discussed the hazards of smoking with the class, show the class a clean cotton ball. Explain that for purposes of the upcoming demonstration, the cotton ball will represent the healthy tissue of a non-smoker's lungs. Allow the students to handle, observe, and pass around the cotton ball.

2. While the cotton ball is being passed around, bring out the "smoker's lung" device. Explain that this contraption will represent a smoker. The cotton ball inside is the lungs. The smoker will smoke one cigarette, and then the class will have the opportunity to observe the damage to the lungs.

3. Light the cigarette. (Be sure to keep the matches out of reach of the students. Also, it is best to do this demonstration near an open window so that the cigarette smoke will be exiting the room. This will decrease the risk of making some students nauseous from the smoke. It may be best to hold the device somewhat outside the window.) Squeeze and release the bottle in a methodical fashion to draw air into the cigarette and thus "smoke" it. Use the jar lid as a makeshift ashtray.

4. After the cigarette has been "smoked" to within about an inch of the bottle nozzle's opening, put the cigarette out by crushing it in the jar lid. Allow the remnants of smoke to escape out the window.

5. Allow students to gather 'round in a central location for purposes of observation. Unscrew the bottle's nozzle and remove the cotton ball (alias "lung tissue").

6. Ask the students, **"How is this cotton ball different from the other cotton ball that you passed around earlier?"** (It has a brown color.) **"What do you think this brown substance is?"** (tar) **"What damage might tar cause in your lungs?"** (lung cancer makes breathing difficult. . .)

Allow students to personally inspect the stained cotton ball.

Smoking (Cont.)

Curriculum Integration

A person who smokes about a pack of cigarettes a day ingests nearly a quart of tar into his/her lungs during the course of a year. A brief lesson introducing liquid measure may accompany "Smoker's Lung." Introduce containers of ounce, cup, pint and quart volumes. Present each container independently from the others so students begin by seeing just the ounce container.

Ask students if they know how much an ounce of liquid is. **"If a product were sold by the ounce, would you need much of it?"** (No.) List some products that are sold by the ounce (perfumes, model paints, food coloring, and so on). Then, bring out the cup container and, using water, fill the ounce container eight times to show that a cup equals eight ounces. The pint container should then be filled by two cup containers. Finally, the quart container should be brought out to be filled by two pint containers.

Have students bring in labels of various products to see in what amounts of liquid measure they are packaged.

Teacher Notes

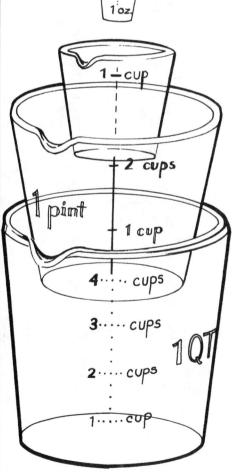

Caffeine

Objective

Students will identify the effects of caffeine on the human body.

Background

This lesson on caffeine has been designed to incorporate the active nature of primary age students with a worthwhile health concept. It allows young students the opportunity to simulate the physical consequences of ingesting caffeine.

Too much caffeine speeds the heart rate and can lead to a loss of appetite or a loss of sleep by stimulating the nervous and circulatory systems. It also increases the need to urinate.

Materials

- several rubber balls or squeeze toys (Two or three for a small number of volunteers will do. However, more will be required if the teacher wants to engage more students at one time.)
- copies of the accompanying worksheets

Preparation

- Obtain the rubber balls or squeeze toys.
- Make a copy of the worksheet for each student.

Procedure

1. Distribute the squeeze toys (or balls) to a select group of student volunteers. (The teacher should have one also.)

2. The instructor should explain that the students' hands and the squeeze toys will represent their hearts and the beating action. "Let's see if we can get our hearts started. IN, OUT. (Squeeze the toy and release.) IN, OUT."

3. Continue by showing how the heart reacts while the body is in various situations. "While we're resting, our hearts will beat in an even relaxed way— IN, OUT; IN, OUT; IN, OUT. (Have students emulate this with their squeeze toys.) The heart is not working too hard. However, when we're playing hard, our hearts will be pumping much faster in order to supply our bodies with oxygen—IN-OUT, IN-OUT, IN-OUT, IN-OUT!" (Squeeze and release the toy more rapidly.) Explain to the class, "It's natural for your heart rate to increase when you exercise hard. It's also natural for it to increase if you become nervous, worried or embarrassed—that's why some people blush when they're embarrassed. (More blood is being pumped through the body to relieve the stress upon it.) Light-colored skin makes this internal process more visible. **If you are resting and not nervous or embarrassed, do you think your heart rate should be slow or fast?**" (slow)

4. "The caffeine in certain foods makes our hearts pump faster even when we're at rest—IN-OUT, IN-OUT, IN-OUT, IN-OUT! **Do you think that's a healthy condition for our hearts?**" (Students should give a negative response.)

5. (Optional) The teacher may assist each student in trying to locate the pulse on their wrist or at their carotid artery near the junction of the jaw and neck. This is more feasible if an aide is available to help reach all the students in a short amount of time.

6. (Optional) After having found their pulses, students could note the difference in heart rate by running in place for a minute or so and then recounting their pulses. (Use a one-minute time period to obtain a pulse rate.) Or just observe the rate change.

7. Pass out the worksheets. Have students mark an **X** on foods they believe to contain caffeine. (chocolate, cola, tea, coffee, chocolate drink mix)

Heart Smart

Place an *X* on the foods that you believe contain caffeine.

Prescription Medicines

Objective

Students will interpret instructions on a prescription drug label.

Background

The parents of primary age students, should always supervise the taking of medicines. Still, young children can be properly trained in reading and following instructions on medicines. They probably won't be able to read (or understand the nature of) the name of the medicine. However, for safety's sake, they should learn to follow the dosage requirements and be alerted to the specific warnings accompanying a particular medication. Such knowledge may increase their respect for medicine in general by helping them to understand that it is only for very specific uses.

As an alternate activity, should the teacher have access to empty prescription bottles, he/she could bring them in for a follow-up evaluation. Number the bottle lids with a marker and create questions similar to the ones found on the worksheet for this activity.

Materials

- the accompanying prescription label examples and student worksheet
- an overhead projector

Preparation

- Make copies of the label sheet and worksheet for each student.
- Make an overhead transparency of the label sheet.

Procedure

1. Begin the lesson with a discussion on the proper use of medicine and the importance of following directions. Pass out the label sheets and corresponding worksheets to each student. (Note the level of reading comprehension involved.)

2. Using the overhead transparency, review the information on one of the labels. Make sure to highlight critical information such as the specific medicine, for whom it is prescribed, proper dosage, and any special warnings.

3. Answer the first two questions as a class before allowing individual students to complete the worksheet on their own.

Answers to Worksheet:

1. two
2. Joe Jones
3. No
4. four
5. No
6. Chew it.
7. Shake it well and take it with food
8. Yes; two refills
9. two
10. for flu symptoms
11. Ask an adult to help

Teacher Notes

_____

_____

_____

_____

_____

_____

_____

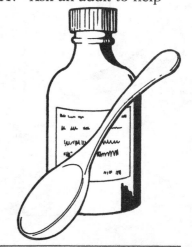

Read Right, Be Safe

(Use with page 46.)

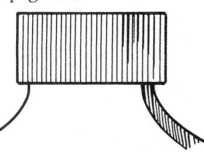

Jones Pharmacy
222 Whitehill Dr.,
Our Town PH:555-5555

RX 325646   **Dr.** REED
Date: 04/13/94   **Name:** Smith, Ann

Take one teaspoonful twice daily.

Clemastine Fumaragener
for Tavist Syrup
*** 2 Refills ***

Downtown Pharmacy
100 Main St.
Your City PH: 555-6666

RX 325688   **Dr.** CHUNG
Date: 08/8/94   **Name:** Jones, Joe

Chew one tablet three times daily until gone.
Amoxicillin
*** No Refills ***

Jones Pharmacy
222 Whitehill Dr.,
Our Town PH:555-5555

RX 352867   **Dr.** Smith
Date: 06/5/93   **Name:** Brown, Bret

Take one teaspoonful four times daily.
120 Advil Suspension
SHAKE WELL. TAKE WITH FOOD.
STORE AT ROOM TEMPERATURE.
*** No Refills ***

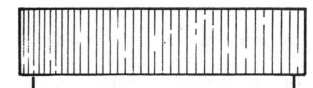

Downtown Pharmacy
100 Main St.
Your City PH: 555-6666

RX 325688   **Dr.** BAKER
Date: 08/8/94   **Name:** Thompson
                              Sharon
Take one capsule twice daily for flu
symptoms.
10 Amantadine Hydrox for Symmetrel
100mg capsules
*** No Refills ***

Read Right, Be Safe

Name _____

(Use with page 45.)

Use the prescription label sheet to answer these questions.

1. How many teaspoons of medicine will Ann Smith take in a day? _____

2. Which person must use all of their medicine for it to work properly?

   _____

3. Can Sharon Thompson get refills on her prescription? _____

4. How many teaspoons of medicine must Bret Brown take every day? _____

5. Should Bret Brown keep his medicine in the refrigerator? _____

6. How should Joe Jones take his medicine? _____

7. What must Bret Brown do every time he takes his medicine?

   _____

8. Can Ann Smith get refills on her prescription? _____

9. How many capsules will Sharon Thompson take in a day? _____

10. Why is Sharon Thompson taking medication? _____

11. If you are not feeling well and think you need medicine, what should you do?

   _____

Over-the-Counter Medicines

Objective

Students will learn to identify the safe use of several common over-the-counter medicines.

Background

Use this lesson after teaching the elements of the safe use of medicine. Modeled after the old Concentration television game show, this lesson's student activity is appropriately used to bring closure to a health text lesson (or unit) on medicine and its proper use.

Materials

- the outer boxes or wrappers of several well-known over-the-counter medicines—aspirin, nasal spray, acetaminophen, eye drops, antiseptic cream, etc.

- transparency sheets (one for each product)

- an overhead projector

- several sheets of construction paper (one for each product)

- the accompanying true/false questions

- clear tape

- the "review" worksheet

Preparation

- Make an enlarged transparency of the front side of a flattened box or wrapper, for use on an overhead. Repeat this for each package that you have.

- Cut a piece of construction paper to cover the flattened box. Then cut this paper into four or five interlocking shapes creating a sort of jigsaw puzzle.

- Number each piece according to its difficulty from 1 to however many total pieces are used to cover the image. (The most obvious puzzle piece clues would have the higher numbers on them. Place #1 over the directions.) Use a little bit of tape to hold each cover piece to the transparency.

- Make a copy of the worksheet for each student.

Procedure

1. Divide students into groups.

2. Explain to the class that on the overhead is the image of a common over-the-counter medicine with which they may be familiar. It is presently covered by several pieces of a jigsaw puzzle. Each group in rotation will be asked a true/false question about the safe use of medicine. (See questions sheet, page 48.) If the group answers the question correctly, they ask to have a specifically numbered piece of the puzzle removed ("We'd like to remove puzzle piece #3."). They then have ten seconds to see if they can identify the mystery medication.

3. If no one correctly guesses the product after ten seconds, the puzzle piece is replaced on the overhead, and the second team is offered a true/false question with the possibility of removing a puzzle piece and correctly identifying the hidden product.

4. When a correct identification of the hidden product is given, that team obtains a point value equal to the sum of the numbered puzzle pieces left on the transparency. If the puzzle originally had four pieces and only pieces #1, #2, and #4 were left on the transparency, that team would score 7 points.

5. Continue the game until either all the true/false questions have been covered or all the images have been identified. The highest score wins.

6. As a review, have each student complete the worksheet.

Answers to Worksheet:

1. pharmacist   2. drug
3. over-the-counter
4. directions   5. prescription
6. true   7. true   8. false
9. false   10. false   11. true
12. true   13. false

Teacher Notes

_____

_____

_____

_____

_____

_____

_____

_____

_____

Concentration

Medicinal Usage Questions with Answers

1. **A medicine should only be taken when people need to get or stay well.** *True*

2. **You should take a medicine whenever you feel the need to take it.** *False. You should always be supervised in the taking of a medicine by either your parents, a nurse, doctor, or other responsible adult.*

3. **Your parents can buy any medicine without a doctor's order.** *False. Some medicines require a physician's prescription.*

4. **A medicine is a drug.** *True.*

5. **Medicines can take the form of a pill, liquid, or cream.** *True.*

6. **Any medicine given to you by a doctor can never harm you.** *False. Some prescription medicines may have harmful side effects, such as a rash or headache, for some people. Be sure to let your parents know if you're not feeling well after receiving a certain medication.*

7. **All medicines should be stored out of the reach of children.** *True.*

8. **You can take medicine that belongs to someone else.** *False. Medicine belonging to others, especially prescription medicine, is designed with their bodies and needs in mind. It may prove harmful to someone else.*

9. **If an over-the-counter medicine is not helpful for a specific illness, check with your doctor as soon as possible.** *True. It may signal a more serious condition that only your doctor could determine.*

10. **A drug is a chemical that changes the workings of your body.** *True.*

11. **A drug can change the way you feel but not the way you think or act.** *False. It can do all three.*

12. **A symptom is a sign from your body that you may be sick.** *True.*

13. **There are medicines that can cure a cold or flu.** *False. Medicines can only help mask the symptoms of a cold or flu.*

14. **An over-the-counter medicine can be bought without a doctor's order.** *True.*

15. **Before taking any over-the-counter medicine, check the inside of the wrapper or carton to see if you've won a prize.** *False. First, read the directions.*

16. **The person who prepares a prescriptive medicine for you is the doctor's nurse.** *False. It is a pharmacist.*

17. **Dentists can order prescriptions for people, too.** *True.*

18. **If a person really isn't feeling well, they can take twice as much of a medication as directed on the label.** *False. Twice the dosage could leave them more ill than they already are. Always follow directions exactly.*

19. **When finished with a particular medicine, it is very important to put it back in its original package.** *True. This way you always know where it is and what's in a specific box/package. Many medicines look alike.*

20. **When you buy an over-the-counter medicine, never buy a box or package that has already been opened.** *True. To be sure that the medicine has not been tampered with in any way, always insist on an unopened container.*

21. **A "side effect" is an undesirable condition due to a drug.** *True.*

22. **The more side effects a medicine gives you, the better it actually is.** *False. Inform your parents immediately so they can talk to your doctor about what to do for you. See #6.*

23. **Your parents need to know about any medicine that you are taking.** *True. They are responsible for you, and they need to supervise any medical treatment for you.*

24. **You should never take two medicines at the same time.** *False. If your doctor prescribes the use of two at once, it is all right. If you are taking a prescription medicine, you probably shouldn't take anything else until your doctor has approved it. Remember, always read labels. Also, be sure to let your doctor know about any medicines you may be taking for another problem.*

Pharmacy Facts

Name _____

Use the Word Bank to fill in the missing word in each sentence. Not all the words will be used.

Word Bank

drug	prescription	directions	pharmacist
dentist	bottle cap	nurse	over-the-counter

1. The person who prepares a doctor's prescriptive medicine is known as a

   _____ .

2. A _____ is a chemical that changes the workings of your body.

3. _____ medicine may be bought without orders from a doctor.

4. One of the first things to do when taking medicine is to read its _____ .

5. _____ medicine can only be ordered by a doctor or dentist.

Write **True** or **False** on the blank line at the beginning of each statement.

_____ 6. A medicine is a drug.

_____ 7. All medicines should be stored out of the reach of children.

_____ 8. You can take medicine that belongs to someone else.

_____ 9. A drug can change the way you feel but not the way you think or act.

_____ 10. If a person doesn't feel well, he/she can take twice as much of a medicine as directed to feel better.

_____ 11. If you have side effects from a particular medicine you need to tell your parents right away.

_____ 12. Medicines can come in various forms—pills, liquids, or creams.

_____ 13. When you take medicine, it's okay to take any amount you feel like taking.

Touch Contamination

Objective

Students will discover important reasons for washing their hands on a regular basis.

Background

This activity has similar objectives to the "Personal Hygiene" lesson on page 54. They complement each other very well. Present this lesson as a teacher demonstration or modify it into a group investigative activity.

Growing mold from the germs on your hands provides a dramatic lesson on the importance of washing hands before eating.

Mold is grown from spores. Spores are tiny bodies that settle on damp food, swell, and reproduce. Different molds have different spores which produce varying colors. The very air we breathe is rich in numerous dust and mold spores. Our body's natural defenses, such as nose hairs and earwax, work to trap such airborne invaders. However, students need to realize that they can decrease the amount ingested by washing their hands regularly.

Materials

- loaf of bread
- two air-tight sandwich bags (the kind that zip)
- water
- measuring tablespoon (or optional graduated cylinder)
- anti-bacterial hand soap
- marker

Preparation

- Obtain all the materials making sure that the bread has been left untouched in its original wrapper.

Procedure

1. Three to four days in advance of the lesson on the importance of washing one's hands, remove a slice of bread from a fresh loaf. With this first slice, your hands should not be clean. In fact, your hands should represent hands that are rarely washed. To achieve this condition, run one of your hands over several dusty areas of your room, and then be sure to handle the initial slice of bread with your dirty hands. Ask a couple of students to handle it as well.

2. Place the contaminated slice into one of the sandwich bags. Before sealing it, add two tablespoons (about 10 ml.) of water to the bag. Mark the bag "Unwashed." (Damp food encourages the growth of mold.)

3. At this point, thoroughly wash your hands (preferably using anti-bacterial soap). Whether this is a teacher-led demonstration or a group activity, it would be timely to do this around lunch time when students may ordinarily be sent to wash their hands.

4. Remove the second slice of bread, taking care to avoid contact with contaminated surfaces. Place it directly into the second sandwich bag. Once again, add two tablespoons of water. Mark it "Washed." Ask the class, **"What is the only difference between what's in these two bags?"** (One slice of bread was handled by dirty hands while the other was handled with clean hands.)

5. Place both bags in a relatively warm, dark area for the next three to four days.

6. To demonstrate the importance of washing hands, remove the two bags for purposes of inspection by the students. The "Washed" bread should have little, if any, mold growing on it. However, the "Unwashed" bread should hold an array of molds. Different colors of mold may even have taken root.

7. Discuss what helped the mold grow on the one slice of bread. (the existence of mold spores, darkness, and moisture) **"Where did the mold spores come from?"** (off numerous surfaces and our hands)

The water represents our body's perspiration (liquid waste that comes through our skin). Germs and dirt can collect more easily on the

Touch Contamination (Cont.)

surface of our skin if the perspiration is not removed through regular and careful washing.

8. Explain to the class, **"In this case we purposely touched many dusty, dirty areas. However, do you think you could pick up a lot of germs during a normal day just by touching things?"** (Yes)

9. Have students take out a piece of paper and list all the things they have touched since the last time they washed their hands. This list probably won't be complete. However, along with the activity, it will get them thinking about the frequency with which they handle objects without washing their

hands. Close with a final question, **"How can we ensure that germs and dirt do not invade our bodies?"** (Wash our bodies daily and our hands regularly throughout the day.)

Teacher Notes

_____

_____

_____

_____

_____

_____

_____

_____

_____

_____

_____

_____

_____

_____

_____

_____

_____

_____

Communicable Disease

Objective

Students will identify five behaviors that help spread communicable diseases.

Background

The lesson's worksheet "Grace Germworthy," is designed as closure for a lesson on disease prevention for younger children (Grades 1,2). For slightly older students (Grades 3,4), it could be used as an anticipatory set to introduce a similar lesson. Students are presented with sound health habits that can break the cycle so often associated with the spread of common communicable diseases such as cold, flu, bronchitis, and so on.

Not sharing another's eating or drinking utensils; not sneezing/coughing upon others; using tissue to blow one's nose; regular hand washings; and keeping one's hands out of one's mouth are basic behaviors that certain younger children have not yet mastered—if not for the lack of a proper role model then for the apparent lack of self-discipline. Obviously Grace Germworthy has not yet caught on to these beneficial habits.

Materials

- copies of the student worksheet

Preparation

- Make a copy of the worksheet for each student.

Procedure

For younger students:

1. Upon completing a lesson on disease prevention (see *Background*), pass out individual copies of the student worksheet. The teacher may group the students in cooperative learning groups, or they may work individually.

2. Read the dilemma aloud to the class, and have each student follow along silently. After reading Grace's pathetic tale, students should answer each of the follow-up questions.

3. The teacher may collect the papers for purposes of evaluation or may conduct a class discussion based on the responses to the questions.

For older students:

Use the worksheet as an anticipatory set.

Answers to Worksheet:

1. She drank from her brother's glass, sneezed on her family, wiped her runny nose with her hand, stuck her finger in her mouth, did not wash her hands before lunch, and shared her lunch.

2. her brother, her entire family, her classmates at school, and especially those who ate with her

3. Grace did not get enough sleep.

Teacher Notes

_____

_____

_____

_____

_____

_____

_____

_____

_____

_____

Grace Germworthy

Grace was slow getting up this morning. The night before, she stayed up past her bedtime, and now she was still very tired. She was so sleepy that she didn't even notice that she had sipped orange juice out of her brother's glass. Neither did he. However, when Grace sneezed without covering her mouth, everyone at the breakfast table had harsh words for her. She felt bad, but she had been daydreaming about being back in her bed.

While on her way to school, Grace's nose began to run as it had for the last day or so. She wiped her hand across her nose and sniffed in deeply. She remembered that today the speaker from the zoo was coming to her class with some special animals. Grace was excited about this.

The speaker from the zoo brought a small monkey for the students to inspect. Grace was so interested in the monkey and the speaker's talk, she didn't realize she had her pinky finger in her mouth the entire time.

When lunch time came, Grace was so hungry she found a way to avoid washing her hands just so she would be first in line. She traded her peanut butter sandwich for her friend's bologna sandwich. (Each friend had already taken a bite.) Again at lunch, Grace wiped her runny nose with the back of her hand. She began to cough. Grace Germworthy wasn't feeling very well.

1. Name five things Grace did that might have passed her germs to someone else.

_____

_____

_____

2. Who else might have gotten sick because of the germs Grace was spreading?

_____

3. What was one thing Grace probably didn't get enough of to help her stay well?

_____

Personal Hygiene

Objective

Students will identify those occasions when it is critical for good health to wash one's hands. They will explain the possible consequences when one does not wash one's hands.

Background

Germs can enter the body through the food or drink we ingest or even through cuts in the skin. But, the most common distribution of germs by far is by the hands. While numerous bacteria and dust are filtered, to a degree, by nose hairs, earwax, and eyelashes as part of the body's built-in defense system, bacteria-laden hands are the one source we have the most control over. Children must acquire the hand-washing habit early on, in order to minimize certain types of bacterial and viral illnesses. (See also the lesson on page 50.)

Materials

- copies of the accompanying student worksheet

Preparation

- Make a copy of the worksheet for each student.

Procedure

1. Present the class with this riddle: **"Can you remember a time when you were given something free by dozens, or maybe even hundreds of people?"** Allow the students to guess several answers before telling them the free-bies they got were germs (bacteria and viruses). "Germs are passed from person to person through the air, especially when someone who has a cold sneezes, or by contact, when one touches something that someone else then touches."

2. Clarify the point made in step #1 by having the students focus on one common object within the school. **"For example, take the doorknob on the door to our class-room. How many of you have touched it today?** If all (or whatever number) of you have touched it, you've been exposed to each other's germs. **Now, how many of you have touched the door-knobs to one of the restrooms (or front en-trance door or office door)?** Think of how many other students have touched those doorknobs. **Are you begin-ning to understand how germs can easily pass from person to person?"**

3. "Not all germs will make a person sick, and our body does have the ability to fight off germs. However, our body needs some help from us. **What part of our body touches more things than any other part of our body?** (our hands) **Do our hands ever come close to the inside of our body?** (Yes, to the mouth, eyes, and nose during times of eating, or sneezing, or other occasions) **How can we be sure that our hands remain as germ-free as possible?"** (Wash them often and at appropriate times.)

4. Pass out copies of the worksheet. After students have completed the activity, review it with them.

Answers to Worksheet:

1. After 2. Before 3. After
4. After 5. After 6. After
7. No Wash 8. Before

Teacher Notes

_____

_____

_____

_____

_____

_____

_____

_____

_____

_____

_____

_____

_____

Enemy at Hand

Name _____

On the line next to each picture write "Before" if you should wash your hands before doing this activity, or "After" if you should wash your hands after doing this activity. If you don't think there is a need to wash your hands before or after a particular activity, write "No."

1._____

2._____

3._____

4. _____

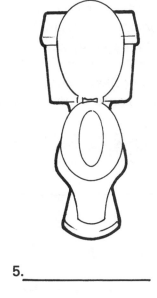

5. _____

6._____

7._____

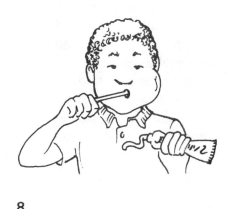

8._____

Posture

Objective

Students will identify the benefits and characteristics of good posture.

Background

Good posture helps the body: by allowing room so organs can grow and function properly; so one can breathe more easily; and by adding to one's personal appearance.

Correct walking posture includes having the back straight, the head up, and the shoulders back. Good sitting posture is characterized by having the feet flat on the floor (the thighs and lower legs making a 90° angle at the knees), the head up and the shoulders back.

Balance an eraser on top of the head (or book when seated) as a reminder to students to keep from slouching. Their posture will be slightly different from that of others, and marching across the room like a soldier on parade is not the goal of good posture. Employing the wall or door in this activity is meant to align the student's body initially, and from that point they are to proceed at a comfortable gait. Factors, such as the shape of a student's head and the speed at which they walk, may cause the eraser to fall even without a slouch.

Materials

- a clean chalkboard eraser
- the student worksheet

Preparation

1. Make a copy of the worksheet for each student.

Procedure

1. After a class discussion on correct posture (see *Background*), ask for a volunteer to demonstrate correct posture with the assistance of an eraser. Each person's posture is a bit different. The volunteer should begin by standing against a totally flat wall or door. The back of his/her head and shoulders down to the rear of his/her calves and heels should be touching the wall. Place the eraser on his/her head, and then have them walk a straight line across the room in a comfortable manner without straining to maintain the rigid position initiated on the wall. Other students may wish to try this. In order to curb confusion and enhance safety, make sure a limited number of students attempt this at one time.

2. Each student may demonstrate correct seated posture by balancing a lightweight book on their head. (See *Background*.)

3. For closure have each student complete the worksheet.

   Answers to Worksheet:
   #'s 1, 2, 4, 5, 8, and 9 should be checked.

Curriculum Integration

This may be an appropriate place to introduce linear measurement by checking each student's height. Use standard or metric measure.

On long sheets of butcher paper, students could team up to create full-size body silhouettes. One student lies flat on the paper while the other carefully traces around his/her body. Students then use a yardstick to draw a straight line from the top of the head, through the center of the torso, to the bottom of the feet. Somewhere on this line they write their name and height.

Teacher Notes

_____

_____

_____

_____

_____

You're No Slouch

Place a check next to each **true** sentence about good posture.

_____ 1. Your head should be up and shoulders back when you walk.

_____ 2. Your feet should be flat on the floor when you sit.

_____ 3. You should walk in a stiff manner like a robot.

_____ 4. Your back should always be straight when you walk.

_____ 5. When you sit, your head, shoulders, and back should be lined up.

_____ 6. When you walk, you should lean forward from the waist.

_____ 7. When you walk or sit, your head should bend slightly forward.

_____ 8. Your posture may be a little different from that of others.

_____ 9. Good posture helps you look your best.

_____ 10. When walking, your shoulders should be slightly rounded.

_____ 11. You must strain and feel somewhat uncomfortable to keep good posture.

Hair and Nail Care

Objective

Students will recognize the importance of keeping one's hair well-groomed and nails clean and neatly trimmed.

Background

Proper grooming of hair requires daily brushing and/or combing to keep it clean and healthy. It requires shampooing the hair at least twice a week to remove accumulated dirt and oil. (Those individuals with more natural oils in their hair will need to shampoo more frequently.) Shampoo should to be worked into the hair and scalp with the fingertips, and then thoroughly rinsed in order to keep the hair from matting together or the scalp from itching.

Nails are to be kept clean by washing regularly and using a nailbrush to remove dirt from under the nails. This is critical because the accumulation of dirt can house numerous germs that could lead to illness. Nails need to be trimmed regularly also. Nails that are too short can become ingrown and very painful. Nails that are overly long are prone to harboring more dirt and breaking off.

Materials

- two used wigs (with Styrofoam head molds, if possible)
- hairbrush
- sink with running water (If you classroom doesn't have this feature, use three plastic dishpans.)
- shampoo
- a large bath towel
- hair dryer

Preparation

- Obtain the two wigs with stands. Friends, relatives, flea markets, and second-hand stores would be the best sources for finding these.
- Obtain the brush, shampoo, dishpans (if needed), towel and hair dryer. The dishpans will be filled with warm water.
- Make a copy of the worksheet for each student.

Procedure

1. Begin with a class discussion on personal grooming of hair and nails. (See *Background*.) Display the two wigs as "Maude" and "Claude." (Any name combination may be incorporated to enliven the lesson. Place each name on the base of the stand for easy future reference.) Explain to the class that one of these two wigs represents the hair of a person who takes good care of his/her hair, while the other symbolizes the hair of a person who doesn't.

2. If your room has a sink with running water, the washing procedure will take place in that location. Otherwise, take one wig and shampoo it in the first dishpan. Rinse it in the second dishpan. Rinse it a second time in the third dishpan, advising the class that this person was always careful to completely rinse soap from his/her hair. Ask the class, **"From our discussion earlier, how often should we wash our hair?"** (at least twice a week)

3. Shampoo the second wig in the first pan. Rinse it in the second dishpan, taking care not to remove all the soap. Explain that this person was in a hurry and didn't take time to get all the soap out of their hair. Ask the class, **"What problems might arise because of this?"** (Hair may mat together; it may be dulled; it can cause the scalp to itch; and dirt and dust can cling to it.)

4. At this point, begin drying each wig by either using a towel and/or a hair dryer. Advise the class that when using a hair dryer, not to use the highest heat setting for a long period of time as it may make hair brittle. When using a towel, pat the hair dry. **Note:** Keep the hair dryer away from water to avoid possible electrical shock.

5. After drying, use the hairbrush to brush the one wig representing proper hair care. Allow the other wig to remain on its stand totally unattended. For the next several days (or weeks), leave the hairbrush out

Hair and Nail Care (Cont.)

for students to give the exemplary wig its daily brushing while totally ignoring the other wig. **Note:** Remind students not to use this hairbrush on themselves. In order to prevent the spread of lice, products designed for haircare, such as brushes or combs, or for use on the head, such as hats, should never be exchanged between individuals. Not wishing to exchange hats or hair care items does not suggest that someone else is unclean. It just says you are careful. Lice can easily be spread to, and from, anyone.

6. Pass out the worksheets. Have students complete them. Students should be able to compare the two wigs on a daily basis. The teacher may wish to shampoo the exemplary wig a second time within the week.

Answers to Worksheet:

1. True   2. True   3. True
4. False   5. False   6. True
7. True   8. False   9. True
10. True

Curriculum Integration

An introductory look at careers may be incorporated with this lesson. If you visit a hair salon on a regular basis, you may be able to persuade a professional hairdresser and/or manicurist to come to your class for a talk detailing further grooming tips and how they became interested in their career.

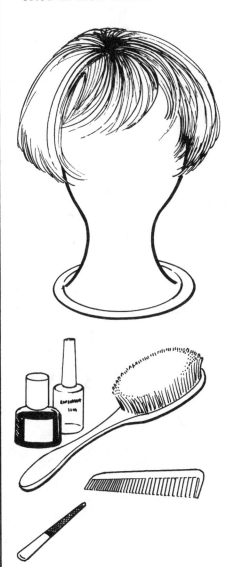

Teacher Notes

_____

_____

_____

_____

_____

_____

_____

_____

_____

_____

_____

_____

_____

_____

_____

Well-Groomed

Name _____

For each of the following sentences, write **True** or **False**.

_____ 1. You should wash your hair at least twice a week.

_____ 2. If you have oily hair, you should wash your hair more often.

_____ 3. Your fingernails and toenails could hold germs if not cleaned.

_____ 4. You should brush your hair every other day.

_____ 5. It is all right to share your hairbrush with anyone.

_____ 6. Biting your nails may harm your fingers.

_____ 7. If you don't properly trim your nails, they may become ingrown.

_____ 8. It is good to have extremely long nails.

_____ 9. Biting your nails could possibly make you ill.

_____ 10. When shampooing your hair, work the shampoo well into your hair and scalp.

On the left hand, draw fingernails that are clean and trimmed. On the right hand, draw fingernails that are not clean and trimmed.

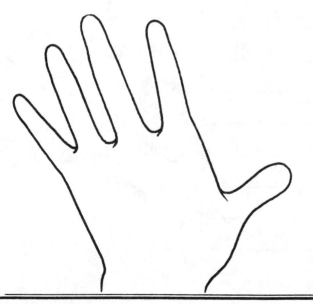

Dental Care

Objective

Students will identify at least four methods of maintaining healthy teeth and gums.

Background

This lesson on dental care may be presented as a teacher demonstration with younger students or as a group activity for older students. The teacher should judge whether or not his/her pupils could safely pour the vinegar and transport the tubs to their overnight location. **In any case, only the teacher should spray the enamel on the eggshells in advance of the activity.**

The first day's lesson should cover all the aspects of proper dental care. (See Step #4 in *Procedure* and the worksheet on p. 63.) The second day, with the physical results of the activity readily apparent to the students, provide reinforcement of the ideas put forth the previous day.

Note: The vinegar will destroy the unprotected shell within a few hours. The enamel-coated shell will probably deteriorate within 24 hours. Keep this timetable in mind when planning and preparing the lesson.

Materials

- the complete shell of an egg (broken in half)
- an empty plastic margarine or cottage cheese tub
- an aerosol can of clear enamel spray
- about four ounces of vinegar
- an old set of tweezers
- copies of the student worksheet

    Note: The above materials (eggshell, plastic tub, and vinegar) are for one teacher demonstration or student group. Provide these items for every participating student group.

Preparation

- The day before the activity, take one of the eggshell halves and spray it inside and out with the clear enamel. While spraying, use the tweezers to hold the shell away from you. Place it broken edge down on some old newspaper to dry. **Caution:** Be sure to use the spray enamel in a well ventilated area or outdoors on a relatively wind-free day.

- Make a copy of the worksheet for each student.

Procedure

1. Begin the demonstration by pouring the vinegar into the small plastic tub. At this point, make the analogy that the acidic vinegar will represent the food one eats and how food sometimes affects the teeth. The eggshells are made of calcium, the same mineral that makes up the teeth and bones in the body. Sometimes bits of food stick to cracks and crevices on the teeth that one doesn't see. When combined with germs present in the mouth, this combination can form acids that attack the enamel, or protective covering, of a tooth. Plaque is the name of the sticky coating that forms on the teeth from this action. It needs to be constantly fought off to keep it from damaging the teeth and gums. Sugary foods are especially prone to forming this destructive coating.

    There are ways to help strengthen the enamel of teeth. (Explain how one eggshell has been treated and relate it to the preventive measures listed in Step #4 below.)

2. Place both eggshell halves into the vinegar. Allow each shell half to sink beneath the vinegar's weight, thereby covering both the interior and the exterior of the shell.

3. Set the tub aside in an undisturbed location overnight.

4. Early the following day, have students check the condition of each shell half. Discuss the outcome. **"What did the vinegar do to the untreated shell half?"** (As an acid, it dissolved the calcium of the unprotected shell.) **"Why did it not affect the other shell?"** (It was protected by the enamel spray.) **"How are our teeth similar to these eggshells?"** (Both are made of calcium.) Note that the enamel will not hold the acid from the calcium indefinitely. Therefore we need to get the acid-causing materials away

Dental Care (Cont.)

from our teeth as soon as possible. **"What are some ways that we can protect our teeth?"** (Brush at least twice a day; limit sugary treats and try to brush after them; floss once a day; see a dentist twice a year; obtain fluoride treatments to strengthen our teeth's enamel; and use a fluoride toothpaste.)

5. Have students complete the worksheet.

Answers to Worksheet:
1. calcium 2. enamel
3. sugary 4. plaque 5. cavity
6. brushing 7. fluoride 8. six
9. toothpaste 10. dental floss

Curriculum Integration

Have a local dentist or dental hygienist come to class to explain how cavities form, discuss proper brushing and flossing techniques, as well as promote other precautionary measures for good dental health. Furthermore, he/she could speak to the students about his/her career in general and the steps taken to realize it.

Teacher Notes

The Hardest Shell

Name _____

Use the Word Bank to complete the following sentences.

Word Bank

enamel	salty	dental floss	toothpaste	toothbrush
calcium	four	brushing	plaque	filling
cavity	six	fluoride	sugary	iron

1. Your teeth are made of _____ .

2. The _____ is the protective covering of your teeth.

3. Foods that stick to your teeth, especially _____ foods, can attack the protective covering of the teeth.

4. _____ is the sticky coating that forms on teeth when food mixes with germs. It can harm the teeth and gums.

5. If the teeth are left unprotected, a _____ or hole may occur in a tooth.

6. You can help your teeth stay healthy by _____ at least twice a day.

7. See your dentist for _____ treatments.

8. You should visit your dentist every _____ months.

9. Use a _____ that contains fluoride.

10. Once a day, clean between your teeth using _____ .

Health-Care Products

Objective

Students will learn how to make an intelligent choice between two competing health-care products based on information available to them.

Background

While many primary students do not control which health-care products are purchased for their home, some do influence the type of toothpaste or hand soap they use by the fact that they *do use it* and their parents relish this fact. Furthermore, in certain other areas, say breakfast cereal or choice of fast food restaurant, many primary students do have inordinate input on the brand or restaurant chosen. Simply put, these youngsters are already flexing some degree of consumer power.

This lesson doesn't focus on the cost aspect of the products presented. It is to be assumed that the costs are similar. Students need to look beyond the glittering slogans, the bandwagon propaganda techniques ("The toothpaste for everyone with a great smile!"), and the celebrity endorsements. With each given pair of products, one has features the other doesn't—fluoride in one toothpaste, bacteria-killing ingredients in one soap, and a recommendation from a professional dental organization for one mouthwash.

Materials

- the accompanying worksheet
- sample magazine ads of health-care products—toothpaste, shampoo, mouthwash, soap, etc.

Preparation

- Make a copy of the worksheet for each student.
- Obtain the magazine ads.

Procedure

1. Share some magazine ads of health-care products with the class. Ask students how these ads try to get people to buy the products. Ask which ads appeal to them. Which ones have more facts to support their claims? (See *Background*.)

2. Pass out the worksheet, and have students individually make their selections.

3. Take the time to close the lesson by discussing the most appropriate choices, making sure that all the students understand the critical facts that determined the wisest choices. Discuss the value of recognizing the unimportant advertising gimmicks.

Answers to Worksheet:
Complete, Pro, and *Excite* would be the preferred choices.

Curriculum Integration

Working in pairs, students could use their language and artistic skills to create ads for fictitious health products. Have several teams do a similar type of product. Place a number on the back of their ads instead of their names. Show these ads to students from a different classroom for the purpose of a preference survey or display in the hallway with ballots. Students would vote on which one of several similar health products they would choose. After the survey, conduct a discussion of the elements contained in the ads that were selected over others.

Teacher Notes

_____

_____

_____

_____

_____

_____

_____

_____

_____

_____

_____

_____

Smart Shopper

Place an **X** next to the health-care product in each pair that you think is better.

Bicycle Safety

Objective

Students will identify eight important rules for bicycle safety.

Background

Thousands of individuals are injured each year riding their bicycles. This lesson helps improve awareness of the safety rules that govern this popular activity. Obviously, it cannot totally ensure that students will transfer classroom knowledge to their neighborhood pavement.

With the proper circumstances, such as an ample parking lot, and cooperation from such organizations as the local police or automobile club, teachers might be able to put together a simulated safety course. Students would then be able to demonstrate their grasp of the bicycle safety rules.

Materials

- the accompanying student worksheet
- a transparency of the bicycle safety tips, "Rules for the Road"
- an overhead projector
- bicycle (optional)

Preparation

- Make a copy of the worksheet for each student.
- Make an overhead transparency of the safety rules and the student worksheet.

- Obtain a bicycle, perhaps one that a student rode to school. (Optional)

Procedure

1. If you have access to a bicycle (make sure it is in good repair), use it as a prop to introduce your lesson on bicycle safety. Ask how many in the class have ever ridden a bicycle. Alert students to the fact that before they ride any bicycle for the first time after an extended period of inactivity (like during the early spring in areas of severe winter), they should have an adult check over their bicycle. Things like correct tire pressure, properly functioning brakes, and a well-oiled chain will allow students to enjoy their bikes longer with less chance of mechanical difficulties or possible injury.

2. Place the "Rules of the Road" bicycle safety guidelines on the overhead and discuss each one with the class.

- Keeping both hands on the handlebars is mandatory to maintain control of the bike.

- Riding double is to be discouraged, since it makes keeping control very difficult for the person manning the handlebars and endangers those positioned directly over the chain.

- Running errands to the store, or wherever, would obviously necessitate the use of a carrying basket. This helps you keep control of the bicycle with two hands and prevents

objects such as a beach towel from falling into the spokes.

- A bicycle is a moving vehicle, and as such, needs to go with the flow of other traffic on the road.

- Hand signals are important so the rest of traffic is aware of the cyclist's intentions (extended left arm for a left turn; extended left arm bent upwards at a 90° angle at the elbow for a right turn).

- Never ride side by side. Due to their slow speeds, bike riders must always stay in single file. Motorized traffic will pass them much more safely in this manner.

- As a part of traffic, obedience to all traffic signs and signals is a must. At busy intersections where multiple lanes of traffic may be moving simultaneously, bicycle riders should walk their bikes across the crosswalks.

- In stretches of road where cars may be parked alongside the curb, riders need to be mindful of the hazards of cars pulling out, backing up, or doors opening.

The final three guidelines are designed to maximize safety wherever and whenever a

Bicycle Safety (Cont.)

student is on a bicycle.

- Long, loose-fitting clothing may get caught within the chain or spokes of a wheel leading to an accident.

- Ill-fitting sandals or bare feet can invite harmful consequences to the toes and feet.

- A helmet is the best protection one can have in case of an accident on a bike since it is designed to protect the most important part of the body from injury. Always wear a helmet!

3. Have students complete the worksheet on page 69.

4. The teacher may collect and individually evaluate each student's paper or may use the overhead transparency to review the activity with the entire class.

Curriculum Integration

Create bicycle safety posters. Individuals or groups of students may plan and create a poster in which they illustrate one of the rules that has been discussed. Assign the rules so each will be covered. Use artistic skills and bright colors to draw attention to the poster's message. Spell accurately and write any words boldly and neatly. Hang the posters in the hallway and encourage students to act as role models for other students in school and in their neighborhood.

Answers to Worksheet:

- a rider going against car traffic

- a rider holding groceries in one hand while trying to steer his/her bike

- a rider crossing his/her bike outside of a designated crosswalk

- two persons riding on one bike

- a rider without a helmet

- a rider running a "Stop" sign

- a rider with his/her head turned backwards so he/she is unaware of a car door opening in front of him/her (from a parked car along the curb)

- a barefoot rider

- a rider with long, loose flowing clothing

- a rider "showing off" with no hands on the handlebars

- two riders going side by side down a busy street

Teacher Notes

Rules of the Road

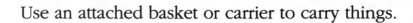

Follow these guidelines for safer fun on your bicycle:

Keep both hands on the handlebars.

Don't ride double.

Use an attached basket or carrier to carry things.

Always ride with the flow of traffic *not against* it.

Use proper hand signals to let others know
your intentions.

When riding with others, stay in a single-file line.
Never ride side by side.

Observe all traffic signs and lights.

When crossing a street, stay in the crosswalk.

Stay alert when riding by parked cars in case drivers pull out
or open their doors.

Avoid wearing long, loose articles of clothing that could
get tangled in the chain.

Don't ride with loose-fitting sandals or barefoot; avoid
injury to your feet!

Always wear a helmet to avoid head injuries.

Bicycle Patrol

Name _____

There are twelve bicycle safety rules being broken in this picture. Can you find them? Circle each one.

Dealing with Strangers

Objective

Students will be able to describe some actions they could undertake when confronted by strangers.

Background

Children are aware of the need to be careful around strangers, but they may not know what to do when confronted by a stranger. Children should never take a chance on a stranger who wishes to either enter their home when the child is alone or take them anywhere. Modify the discussion to fit the needs, ages, and fears of your students. The use of a password system by which children can identify their parents' actual desires may be initiated. It may prove helpful to provide role-playing opportunities for groups of students in which they act out a discussion with their parents on setting up a password system.

Materials

- the accompanying student worksheet

Preparation

- Make a copy of the worksheet for each student.

Procedure

1. Discuss "strangers" with the class. Help them realize that a stranger is anyone they do not know *well*. There are those strangers whom they have never seen before, as well as strangers whom they may have seen or perhaps even met once before. The key is that they do not know them well. While the majority of strangers will never mean them any harm, they must be prepared to "play it safe" at all times.

2. Ask students to think of times when they might be at risk from a stranger who may mean them harm (when they are alone, at home, or in the neighborhood). Review some basic guidelines to follow in these situations. **At home:** "Never allow strangers into your home. If your parents are home, keep the door locked and tell your parents someone's at the door. If you're alone, keep the door locked and don't answer it. If a stranger calls on the phone, tell the caller that your father or mother is busy at the moment and that you can take a message. Never tell a stranger that your parents aren't home." **Away from home:** "Never go anywhere with a stranger. Don't get into his/her car or be enticed to go anywhere with someone you don't really know. Talk to your parents about arranging a code, or password, by which you would know for sure the person coming to pick you up at school or ball practice was really sent by your parents. Be aware of your neighborhood. Know where 'block homes' are in case you need to run to one when you think someone might harm you."

3. Read the vignettes on the worksheet aloud, while students follow along silently. Either working in small groups or as a whole class, discuss the appropriate action to take in each situation.

Possible Answers for Worksheet:

1. Patrick may ask Bob for the family password. If he doesn't know it, or if there is no password, Patrick should go to the office and let school officials make some calls.

2. While there may be some truth to the man's story, Tina should not stick around to find out. She should walk away from the man in the direction of other people in the park, toward a nearby 'block home,' or toward her house, whichever offers the most immediate refuge.

3. Fred should, under no conditions, approach the car. He should continue walking directly home or go to the nearest 'block home'. Fred should also be advised to buddy-up on his way to and from school.

4. Rhonda should not answer the door. The door ought to be locked. She should remain out of sight. The presence of a person in a uniform is not necessarily the signal to open a door. If indeed it is the gas company, representatives can contact her parents later.

Play It Safe!

1. Patrick is just about to leave school when a man walks up to him at the school door. Patrick recognizes him as Bob, somebody his dad knows. Bob tells Patrick that Patrick's father wants him to go with Bob to pick up Patrick's mother who had to take the family car to the repair shop. Bob says since Patrick's mother won't be home, and she needs a ride home as well, Bob decided to pick up both Patrick and his mother. *What should Patrick do?*

_____

_____

2. Tina is playing with a few friends at the park. After a while, her friends leave, but Tina wants to enjoy the swings for just a bit longer. A man comes up to her and tells her he has found an injured dog not far from the park. He wants Tina to come with him to help the dog. *What should Tina do?*

_____

_____

3. Fred is walking down one of the side streets in his neighborhood on his way home from school. A car pulls up close to the curb, and the driver motions to Fred from his window. The driver calls to Fred to come over to his car saying, "Son, I need some help finding a certain address. Would you show me where I am on this map I have?" *What should Fred do?*

_____

_____

4. Rhonda is home alone. Her parents are out on an errand and will be back within one-half hour. A man knocks at the front door. Rhonda has never seen this person before, but he is wearing a uniform. He says "Gas Company" as he knocks on the door. *What should Rhonda do?*

_____

_____

Home Accident Prevention

Objective

Students will identify preventable home accidents.

Background

Each year tens of thousands of Americans are injured to varying degrees in preventable home accidents. Most of these incidents involve falls and, in the case of small children, accidental poisonings. The "Safe at Home" worksheet attempts to have students reflect upon personal responsibilities that could affect safety within their home. While their parents may or may not indulge in a careless moment from time to time, it is the student's own behavior that he/she needs to focus upon.

The teacher will simulate household hazards in the classroom, using the following seven items and the accompanying rationales: the aspirin bottle needs to be out of reach of small children to avoid accidental poisoning. A child-proof medicine cabinet or cupboard would do the trick. For similar reasons, toxic household products should also be stored in a child-proof cupboard or storage area. Unprotected electrical outlets need to be covered to keep small children from incurring electrical shock by placing wet fingers or metallic objects in the outlet. The stepladder with toy is an open invitation for small children to climb and possibly fall. Such ladders need to be used for their intended purpose and then promptly put in a proper storage place. The appliance by the bathtub is an opportunity for possible electrical shock. Never allow electrical appliances of any sort to be operated near a bathtub, sink or shower with running water. Also, never operate electrical appliances with wet hands. Scattered toys are a veritable minefield over which anyone could fall and cause injury to him/herself. Every toy needs to have its proper storage place after it has been used. Finally, the unmarked container is a potential danger just because it is unknown. Although there are equal chances that it is benign, the same odds hold for it being hazardous. Leave labels on all containers, especially those with toxic contents.

Materials

- an empty aspirin bottle
- the label from a cleaning solution, toilet bowl cleaner, or other toxic household product (Try to get one distinctly marked "Poison".)
- two cylindrical oatmeal boxes
- construction paper (optional)
- an electrical outlet safety cover
- an assortment of about a half-dozen small toys
- a small stepladder
- an electrical appliance (A hair dryer would be ideal.)
- a 2' x 3' posterboard or butcher paper outline cutout of a bathtub
- the accompanying student worksheets
- (optional) a filmstrip or short video tape on household safety (A pre-recorded segment of a network program such as *Rescue 911* may be appropriate.)

Preparation

- Obtain the various items listed.
- Remove the original labels from both oatmeal boxes or cover them with construction paper. Tape or glue the label of the toxic household product around the outside of one of the boxes. The other oatmeal box will be left unmarked.
- Make a rough outline of a bath tub from the posterboard and label it "Bathtub."
- Position the items in the following manner in an area limited to about one-half of your classroom: set the aspirin bottle and the toxic product box on some low tables or chairs (separated from each other); place the safety cover on only one-half of an electrical outlet; place the stepladder along the perimeter of the area you're working in with a toy of some sort on top of it; attach the bathtub outline along a chalkboard or wall with the electrical appliance plugged into an outlet very close to the tub; scatter the remaining toys on the floor nearby, but not directly within, a traffic pattern

in your room; and place the second unmarked oatmeal box somewhere in the area where no other hazards have been placed.

Procedure

1. Spark your student's interest in a lesson on household accident prevention. Can they identify the precarious situations you have created in the classroom? Working in teams of three or four, have each group make its way quietly around the area which you have created.

2. Then, meeting in their groups, discuss the accident situations each group recognized. Have each person record those that their group identified. Each person should write why he/she thinks a certain situation could be a potential accident.

3. As an alternative way to manage, have each group browse independently through the area, while the rest of the class is occupied with either a teacher-led discussion of student experiences with household accidents or the viewing of a tape or filmstrip on the topic.

4. After all groups have finished, focus a class discussion on: which situations were identified as possible safety hazards; why they were so identified; and how an accident could be avoided. Make sure the groups have listed the proper seven items before going further in the discussion.

5. As a review, have each student complete the "Hazards at Home" worksheet.

6. Pass out the "Safe at Home" worksheet to each student, explaining that they should use the charts over the next two weeks to see if they are helping to make their home a safer place. Read over each item on the list together to make sure everyone understands what they are to be checking at home.

Teacher Notes

Hazards at Home

The Hazards' home is very dangerous. They are not very careful people. See if you can find the ten possible dangers lurking in the picture below. Circle each one you find.

Safe at Home

Each evening for the next two weeks, answer each of the following questions by placing a **Yes** or **No** in each day's box. Have a parent or guardian initial the boxes each week.

I have picked up all toys and other items that I used and stored them properly.

	Sun.	Mon.	Tues.	Wed.	Thurs.	Fri.	Sat.
1st Week							
2nd Week							

I have kept the stairs in my home free of my things.

	Sun.	Mon.	Tues.	Wed.	Thurs.	Fri.	Sat.
1st Week							
2nd Week							

I have asked permission to use and have returned harmful products (cleaners, medicines, and so on) to their proper locations.

	Sun.	Mon.	Tues.	Wed.	Thurs.	Fri.	Sat.
1st Week							
2nd Week							

I have not used electrical applicances near water.

	Sun.	Mon.	Tues.	Wed.	Thurs.	Fri.	Sat.
1st Week							
2nd Week							

Water Safety

Objective

Students will identify six important rules of safe swimming.

Background

Play this game after discussing pool safety. Nothing compares with competent swimming instruction for preparing kids to safely enjoy the water. Obviously, the classroom is not going to be a "hands-on" environment for this topic. However, the lesson is designed to help reinforce the cognitive aspects of safe swimming. Such a review will give students cause to think before they leap into a risky situation involving water. Play the game until all situations have been covered, even though one team may be finished.

Materials

- various colored markers
- an overhead projector
- the accompanying sheets of swimming situations, pool illustration, and review
- one die

Preparation

- Make an overhead transparency of the lap pool illustration.

Procedure

1. Divide the class equally into two to four teams.

2. On a rotating basis present each team with a different swimming situation. Allow time for teams to discuss and reason out the scenario. If they offer a correct response to the situation, roll the die to see how many yards they may travel down the pool lane. (Each dot on the die represents 10 yards.) Use the colored markers to keep track of each team's advances. The first team to reach the finish line wins. This game can be modified for small group play.

3. As a review, have students complete the "Swim Team Review" worksheet.

Answers to Worksheet:

1. lifeguard   2. swim
3. drown   4. electrocuted
5. tired   6. head-first
7. run   8. high dive
9. "No Swimming"
10. dangerous

Teacher Notes

_____

_____

_____

_____

Water-Safety Game Questions

- A friend of yours wants you to go swimming with him at his grandparents' farm pond. Your friend says his parents will take you both to the farm whereupon they will leave with the grandparents to go shopping. Your friend says it will be great because you'll have the farm pond all to yourselves. What should you do? *Swimming without a lifeguard or another supervising adult can be very dangerous. Express your concerns about the swim and don't swim unless proper supervision is present.*

- You're at the local community pool with your family on a Sunday afternoon. Your father is already in the pool at the shallow end. He calls for you to step into the water and join him. You are not a good swimmer yet. What do you do? *Join him. Even if you can't swim, you're at the shallow end and in the company of a parent and surrounding lifeguards.*

- You are a good swimmer and live near a shallow stream. Recent rains have increased the amount of water in the stream to a point where a swim would be splendid. What should you do? *Never swim alone. Never swim in a rain-swollen river or stream. The current could be strong enough to drown you.*

- You are at a friend's house enjoying their backyard pool. Your friend's parents have been keeping an eye on the two of you for safety's sake. You begin to see dark clouds approaching and you hear thunder. What should you do? *Never stay in water when thunder or lightning is present. Should lightning strike the water, it could electrocute you since it travels through water.*

- After an early afternoon baseball game, you went to the community pool around 3:00. It's now 5:30, and you have been swimming for over two hours. You begin to feel tired. What should you do? *If you feel tired, get out of the water before fatigue causes possible muscle cramps which could keep you from getting out of the water safely.*

- You are with friends investigating the abandoned rock quarry on a hot Saturday morning. At one part of the quarry, combined groundwater and rainwater have created a beautiful pond. Although a nearby sign says, "No Swimming," your friends think it would be neat to swim in it. After all, everyone is wearing shorts. They say anyone who doesn't swim is a "chicken." What should you do? *The sign is there for a reason. The water is probably very deep, and there is the added danger of submerged rocks. Explain that to your friends, and don't go in.*

- You're playing ball tag in the community pool with a group of friends. The ball bounces off your shoulder and falls into deeper water behind you. Your swimming skills aren't great and the ball is now where the water is over your head. What should you do? *Let someone else who can swim better get the ball. Deep water can wait until your swimming skills improve.*

- It's really hot, and you can't wait to get into the pool. You always swim in the shallow end where the water isn't over your head. You're thinking about diving in to cool down fast. What should you do? *Don't ever dive headfirst into shallow water. You could damage your neck and possibly injure your spinal cord and suffer paralysis. Wade into the pool first, then enjoy the water.*

- You and your friend have just arrived at the crowded local community pool and removed your sandals. After applying some sunscreen, you're friend shouts out, "Last one in is a rotten egg!" and sprints across the wet concrete pavement toward the pool's edge. What should you do? *Be a rotten egg. Don't run in congested areas on a concrete surface near a body of water. One slip of either foot may cause you to fall and crack your head on the side of the pool.*

- **You join some friends at a neighbor's pond to go swimming. Several parents have agreed to supervise your group although none of them have ever gone swimming in this pond. There is a small hill on one side of the pond. You and your friends are tempted to use this hill as a place from which to dive into the pond. What should you do?** *Never dive from or into a location that you know nothing about. Someone, preferably an adult, should check out the pond below the hill. It must be deep enough with no submerged rocks, trees or other obstructions. Again, you must think about protecting your neck.*

- **Even though you can't swim very well, you are enjoying a day at the local pool when a friend dares you to join him/her on the high dive. Your friend says it would be "awesome" and "if you're not a sissy, you'll jump off." What should you do?** *The high dive is obviously located above very deep water. It is not intended for those with limited swimming skills. Be smart, stay safe, perhaps find a new friend.*

- **You are on vacation with your family and have stopped at a motel to spend the night. You and your sister have pestered your parents into letting you go swimming before your family goes out to eat. After you unpack and put on your swimwear, you and your sister tear down the hall toward the motel's pool. When you get there, there is no lifeguard on duty and no one else around. What do you do?** *Check signs to see if a lifeguard will be on duty. At any rate, do not enter the pool until an adult (probably your parents) can supervise you.*

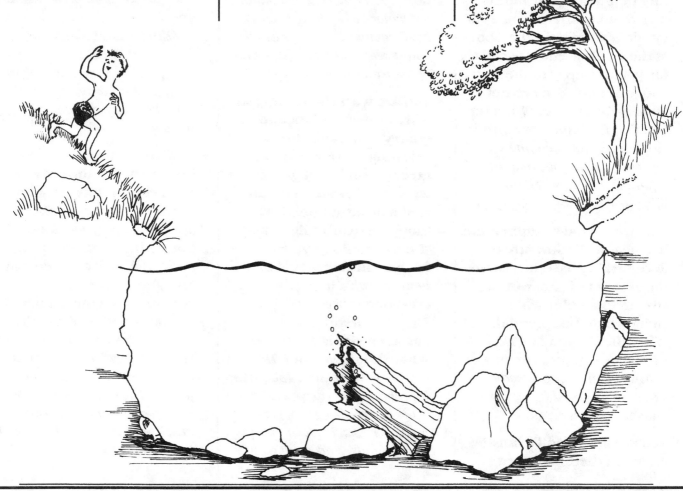

Lap Pool

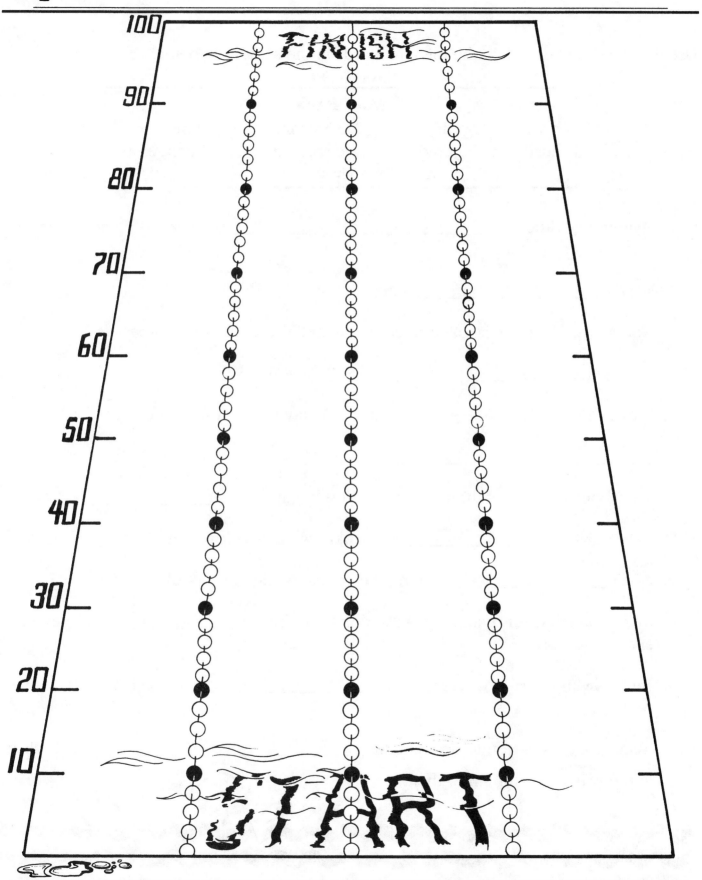

Swim Team Review

Name _____

Use the Word Bank to fill in the missing words in the sentences below.

Word Bank

high dive	drown	"No Swimming"	lifeguard
head-first	tired	electrocuted	dangerous
	run	swim	

1. Swimming without a _____ or supervising adult can be very dangerous.

2. Never _____ alone.

3. Never swim in a rain-swollen river or stream . The current could be

   strong enough to _____ you.

4. When thunder or lightning is present, don't stay in the water. You could be

   _____ .

5. You should get out of the water when you begin to feel _____ .

6. Never dive _____ into unknown or shallow water.

7. Don't _____ along the concrete edge of a pool.

8. If you have limited swimming skills, don't use the _____ at the deep end of the pool.

9. Never swim in water where _____ signs have been posted.

10. If someone dares you to do something _____ or foolish in the water, don't listen to them.